REFINER'S FIRE

The Struggle and Triumph of John the Baptist

Tools for Navigating Doubt, Reclaiming Your Faith, and Discovering the Gospel All Over Again

RACHEL STARR THOMSON

Refiner's Fire: The Struggle and Triumph of John the Baptist
Tools for Navigating Doubt, Reclaiming Faith, and Discovering the Gospel All Over Again

Published by 1:11 Publishing
An imprint of Little Dozen Press
Crystal Beach, ON, Canada
littledozen.com

Copyright © 2020 by Rachel Starr Thomson

Visit the author at rachelstarrthomson.com.

For bulk order information or for more information about 1:11 Ministries, visit one11ministries.com.

Unless otherwise noted, all Scripture quotations are taken from the Holman Christian Standard Bible®, Copyright © 1999, 2000, 2002, 2003, 2009 by Holman Bible Publishers. Used by permission. Holman Christian Standard Bible®, Holman CSB®, and HCSB® are federally registered trademarks of Holman Bible Publishers.

Scriptures marked "NKJV" are taken from the New King James Version®. Copyright © 1982 by Thomas Nelson. Used by permission. All rights reserved.

Scriptures marked "ESV" are taken from The ESV® Bible (The Holy Bible, English Standard Version®). ESV® Text Edition: 2016. Copyright © 2001 by Crossway, a publishing ministry of Good News Publishers. The ESV® text has been reproduced in cooperation with and by permission of Good News Publishers. Unauthorized reproduction of this publication is prohibited. All rights reserved.

Scriptures marked "KJV" are taken from the Holy Bible, King James Version. Public domain.

All Rights Reserved. This book, or any portion thereof, may not be reproduced or transmitted in any form or by any means, electronic or mechanical, including photocopying, recording, or by an information storage and retrieval system (except by a reviewer, who may quote brief passages in a review or other endorsement, or in a recommendation to be printed in a magazine, newspaper, or on the Internet) without written permission from the publisher.

ISBN: 978-1-927658-53-6

Dedication

To Michelle Renee Wade.
You've always asked the best questions,
refused to accept lousy answers,
and believed I would someday raise a ruckus.
This book is dedicated to you.

Acknowledgments

Without question, the references in this book are too few. Wherever I was conscious of a specific debt, I tried to give credit where credit is due. For this project, it is especially due to N.T. Wright, whose work has helped me put my own studies into a helpful framework and provided important insights I wouldn't have reached on my own. Dallas Willard was a significant influence on this book as well. And I would not have explored many aspects of John's story and the theology it suggests without years of conversation with my dear friend Mercy Hope. But anything I know, I know only because of the work of others who have come before me—apostles and prophets, theologians, pastors and priests, missionaries, translators, thinkers and scholars, writers, professors, true friends, and ordinary believers.

If this book is anything, I hope it isn't original. Thank you, all of you, for laying out a path for me to follow.

Table of Contents

Introduction	9
1 The Question from Prison	15
2 A Quick Interlude on the Nature of Faith	27
3 What John Believed: The Story of Israel and the One to Come	35
4 What John Believed: Messiah, Son of David	65
5 What John Believed: The Apocalypse of Daniel	77
6 The Messenger	105
7 The Bend in the Road: When Everything Goes Sideways	135
8 The Gospel That Subverts Expectations	147
9 The Way Through: Choosing Faith Over Doubt When There Are Reasons for Both	177
10 The Apologetics of Experience	217
11 Wisdom Is Vindicated by Her Children	237

Introduction

This is not a book I ever intended to write. It began as an obligation to pen a few thoughts on the story of John the Baptist in Matthew 11 as part of a much longer series on the gospel of Matthew as a whole, written and published for my blog. I had no special attachment to the story in Matthew 11 and frankly just wanted to crank something out and move on. But sometimes life, and writing, takes an unexpected turn.

As I wound down the end of my study of Matthew 10, I looked ahead to chapter 11 with the intention of skipping fairly quickly over the interaction between Jesus and John the Baptist. That would allow me to get back to the actual teachings and actions of Jesus, where I really wanted to dig in.

But instead, I found myself writing an outline for an entire series within the Matthew series, or, as I came to think of it, a book within the blog. That book is what you are reading now.

I didn't mean to write a book about John the Baptist, and frankly, when I sat down to do it, I had at least three other book-sized projects clamoring for my attention. But I couldn't shake the sense that I needed to stop and delve deeply into this story, and that I needed to do it immediately. I couldn't shake the sense that someone needed it.

Interestingly, just days after I started this project, several high-profile defections took place within the evangelical church world—outspoken and prominent Christian leaders who declared they were leaving not only the church but also Jesus. That is heartbreaking, but I didn't begin this project in response to them. If my words can be of help to anyone impacted by those events, I am grateful to the Holy Spirit for it.

So, Matthew 11, beginning in verse 1:

> When Jesus had finished giving orders to His 12 disciples, He moved on from there to teach and preach in their towns. When John heard in prison what the Messiah was doing, he sent a message by his disciples and asked Him, "Are You the One who is to come, or should we expect someone else?"
>
> Jesus replied to them, "Go and report to John what you hear and see: the blind see, the lame walk, those with skin diseases are healed, the deaf hear, the dead are raised, and the poor are told the good news. And if anyone is not offended because of Me, he is blessed."

As these men went away, Jesus began to speak to the crowds about John: "What did you go out into the wilderness to see? A reed swaying in the wind? What then did you go out to see? A man dressed in soft clothes? Look, those who wear soft clothes are in kings' palaces. But what did you go out to see? A prophet? Yes, I tell you, and far more than a prophet. This is the one it is written about:

> Look, I am sending My messenger ahead of You;
> he will prepare Your way before You.
>
> "I assure you: Among those born of women no one greater than John the Baptist has appeared, but the least in the kingdom of heaven is greater than he. From the days of John the Baptist until now, the kingdom of heaven has been suffering violence, and the violent have been seizing it by force. For all the prophets and the Law prophesied until John; if you're willing to accept it, he is the Elijah who is to come. Anyone who has ears should listen!"[1]

There's something undeniably rough-edged about this interaction. At the height of Jesus's public ministry, just when he was beginning to expand and send out his apostles, his cousin—also the man who was largely responsible for launching Jesus's ministry—very publicly expressed doubt. John, who had once declared that he was not worthy to untie Jesus's sandals, now indicated his own fears that he might have chosen the wrong man to follow.

It's painful. If we dare put ourselves in John's shoes, it's frightening. And it may be familiar.

Our reasons for doubt are many. They can be broad. We encounter reasons to doubt our faith, and our God,

---

1 Matthew 11:1–15

in school, on the street, and in the media. The world around us is in many ways post-Christian, and it does its best to push us toward unbelief.

The influences we encounter include social pressures, among them changing sexual mores and repeated calls to reexamine our history[2]—calls which typically conflate Christianity with Colonialism. We may find ourselves put off by the discomfort and antagonism of the current political climate, or growing more and more uncomfortable within our particular religious context, be it evangelicalism or another strain of the Christian faith. Other reasons for doubt may include the influence of religious pluralism, the popular concept of "spirituality without religion," or the cult of rationalism.

Or they may be deeply personal. We may find ourselves doubting not because of the media or the slant of a particular college course, or because of pressure to bend to a culture that seems determined to shame and chastise nearly everyone who believes anything, but because we feel personally let down by God, or even abandoned by him.

The fallout of doubt is sometimes very private and sometimes very public, but either way, when it's left unaddressed it can be incredibly damaging. We might

---

[2] To be abundantly clear, I think this reexamination can be necessary, especially when we're asked to reassess our history through a lens of social justice and equality. God has always been on the side of the oppressed, and Colonialism has always tended to conflate its own desire for power and supremacy with righteousness and the will of God. But a massive deconstruction such as we are undergoing as a society does tend to shake *everything*, deservedly or not, and collateral damage is real.

walk away from the faith entirely—or we might just quietly, privately stop trusting the God we still profess.

That's the biggest reason this book exists. We rarely talk about the creeping pain of doubt, about our own fears that we might be wrong, or self-deluded, or borderline crazy. We rarely talk about the need we feel to put up defenses against questions that hit too close to home. Yet this experience—of doubt and disappointment, or at its height, a crisis of faith—is common to everyone who tries to live by faith, and it's something I think we should bring into the light.

I know too many people who have faced crises of faith and felt alone. I've watched too many fall away from the faith, while family, friends, and followers are left to pick up the pieces. The question John asked, and the doubt and disappointment that drove it, are not strangers to us today. We still ask these questions, if we dare. We still feel these feelings, though we may not feel free to express them.

This book does not offer all the answers, not by any stretch. It is not a book of apologetics, and as you'll see as you read, it is written from a starting point of belief, not of skepticism. It is written from one pilgrim who wants to be faithful to other pilgrims who want to be faithful—or at least, who don't feel quite ready to give up on the faith they have walked in thus far.

Birthed as it was in the study of Matthew, this book is part Bible study and part conversation. It uses the story of John the Baptist to examine the nature of faith and doubt, and to explore the mysterious and sometimes confounding contours of the gospel. Finally, it offers perspectives on faith in the modern world and in our modern hearts.[3]

I hope this book will do several things. I hope it will give us freedom to ask questions and to express our fears and doubts. I don't think we are served by stuffing these things away. More than that, I hope it will give the shaking, the rocked, and the devastated tools to process their questions and feelings and to channel them toward restoration and solid ground. I hope it will give us new frameworks and ways of thinking about our faith that can sustain us better than the old ways did, and that it can point us in truly helpful directions for the journey.

And of course, I hope it will enable us all to delve more deeply into the story of Jesus and the kingdom of God, as the Bible tells it.

Thanks for coming along.
Rachel Starr Thomson
March 2020

---

[3] I'm using "modern" here in the sense of "contemporary," not in the sense of modernism.

Chapter 1:
The Question from Prison

"Are you the One who is to come, or should we expect someone else?"

The question hung in the air that day, its power arresting. Asked publicly, it must have caused every group present to lean in for the answer.

There were the askers—the disciples of John the Baptist, who had delivered the question on his behalf. John, their rabbi, was in prison, where he was in danger of his life.

There were Jesus's own disciples, men and women who had chosen to follow him presumably believing that he was "the One who is to come." The phrase meant the Messiah (Greek "Christ"), the deliverer of Israel, whose presence lay beneath all the prophetic Hebrew Scriptures and yet remained, in some respects, shrouded and mysterious.

Jesus was likewise mysterious. He spoke and acted like a direct representative of Yahweh, Israel's God, whom he called "Father." But to this point, he had never openly declared himself to be the Messiah.

His disciples were putting their faith in a man who

was strangely cagey about who he really was. But now John's disciples were forcing the issue.

And there were the others. The crowds—the "multitudes," to use the classic English wording of the King James Bible. The people who came, sick and crippled, to be healed. The people who came, poor and oppressed, to find hope. Mingled among them were the curious, the questioning, and the outright hostile.

REASONS FOR BELIEF

When it came to Jesus's identity as the Messiah, there were three primary reasons people believed.

To go from the broad to the specific, the first was national expectation within the signs of the times. The Old Testament prophets had pointed to a long period of exile and oppression for Israel, beginning with Babylon and culminating in the iron rule of an empire more powerful than any that had come before it. The dominance of this empire would be followed by the rise of the Messianic kingdom—and the Messianic kingdom, in turn, would crush the iron empire.

By the time of Jesus, the exile had extended over five hundred years.[1] For multiple reasons, the Roman Empire was an obvious fulfillment of the iron empire. It seemed, therefore, that the age of the Messiah was at hand.

---

[1] Some of the Israelites did return to their own land after seventy years in Babylon, as the prophet Jeremiah predicted, and they rebuilt the temple at that time. But as N.T. Wright has pointed out in many places, the period of "exile" continued in that they remained under the domination of foreign powers. See for example N.T. Wright, *The Day the Revolution Began* (New York: HarperOne, 2016).

The second was Jesus's obvious power and authority. He healed people. He worked miracles. He taught about the kingdom of God, and his words had an unusual freshness and an unusual weight. He was also a descendant of David, a direct heir to the ancient royal line. He was, therefore, a good candidate for the Messiah.

But the third and most immediate reason people believed Jesus might be the Messiah, the reason many had begun following him in the first place, was the influence of John the Baptist. John had come out of the desert years before blazing with zeal, filled to overflowing with the Holy Spirit, and calling people to repentance, faith, and baptism in preparation for the Messiah's coming. A prophet who seemed to have stepped straight out of the Old Testament, he captured the public imagination and fired their hearts, convincing nearly everyone that he had been sent by God. And John had—very—publicly declared that Jesus was the One.

But now he sent a question from prison calling Jesus to account.

Remember, it was John who had launched Jesus into ministry. John's entire life work, his credibility as a prophet, and his conception of himself as a man of God hung on Jesus's answer.

SHOULD WE EXPECT SOMEONE ELSE?

John's question possesses a tone that, two thousand years later, we can still hear. It sounds ... hurt? Offended? Perhaps demanding? Affronted and affronting?

We may hear in John's voice a mix of emotions we are rarely comfortable openly expressing toward God: anger and vulnerability chief among them.

By the time John sent his question, Jesus had remained noncommittal about his Messiahship for roughly two years. His ministry bore some of the marks of the Messiah, as they had been identified and defined through the Old Testament Scriptures. But it seemed to lack others. In particular, Jesus showed little proclivity to pick up the sword and begin leading the charge against Rome. Nor did he seem to care quite enough about repentance and holiness among God's chosen people. And lately he had been openly nihilistic—an incredibly confusing stance for a man who was expected to triumph over Rome and renew the people of God.

Of course, all of these things could be misunderstandings or just matters of timing. Perhaps John wasn't hurt or doubting so much as he was justifiably impatient. With so much on the line, he simply wanted to know that he'd gotten things right. Perhaps he was simply asking Jesus to stop dancing around the issue and give him a straight answer.

Some have suggested that John was not really questioning Jesus's Messiahship at all, and that he sent his disciples to Jesus with this question for their own sake. And this is possible. It's also possible that he was trying to push Jesus into openly declaring himself for the sake of getting the whole show on the road, so to speak.

But when I read this story, I find the issues of anger and vulnerability, confusion and doubt far more compelling.

After all, whether we're willing to admit it publicly or not, we all deal with questions and confusion at some point in our Christian lives.

Most of the time, if we are people of faith at all, we believe we know what God is doing. There are two parts to that: we believe we know *what God is doing*. And we believe *we know*.

Those two certainties—that God is doing what we think he's doing, and that our understanding of what he's doing is correct—are pillars we build our lives upon.

But sometimes the pillars shake.

Sometimes God gives us a promise and doesn't keep it.

(Or so it seems.)

Sometimes we step out in faith and fall flat on our faces.

Sometimes we lose our certainty. New questions arise. Our understanding matures, broadens, and old sureties no longer look sure. Tragedies shake us. Leaders fall away. Friends take a different road. Spouses or children leave. The sick die. Black and white bleed into grey.

Doubts take root.

We start to wonder.

Are you really the One?

Or should we look for someone else?

The Fearful Truth

In all this we feel things we've never felt toward God before. Things we are afraid to express. Anger. Unbelief. *Disappointment.* (So awful it has to be whispered.) We feel a frightening fragility. We are offended. We feel hurt.

Or we feel nothing at all. And that is even worse.

Doubt, anger, disappointment—the experience of these things easily boils into a crisis of faith.

I'm not sure, in a visible and tangible world where we trust in the invisible and intangible, that crises of faith can be avoided, or even that they should.

Would we really be sane, or credible, if we never had them?

John the Baptist was a forerunner. He came to prepare the way for Jesus. He came to go first. In this one area, perhaps he also went before *us*. Maybe a crisis of faith is a rite of passage, one every believer must undergo at some point.

John believed.

More ardently, actively, and zealously than anyone else in his day.

And then, for a few terrifying hours or days—or maybe weeks, maybe months or even years before he ever expressed his fear—he wasn't sure if he believed anymore.

In such moments, everything we thought was certain becomes open to question. The ground shakes beneath us. Our souls shake.

When John sent his question to Jesus, he was in prison. He had stood up against the corrupt rulers of the day and suffered for it. He'd also heard that Jesus had begun expanding his ministry by appointing and sending out apostles in his name, and that he'd promised his apostles little but loss, hardship, and persecution. He *hadn't* promised them the victory Messianic Scriptures pointed toward. Instead he had said they would face the loss of everything, including their lives, but would be rewarded eternally for allegiance to him.[2]

And while we can't know exactly what was going on in John's head when he heard these things, his question to Jesus indicates that he was no longer completely convinced he'd been right when he declared Jesus was the Messiah. Something in what Jesus said or did, or didn't say or didn't do, raised real doubt.

John, The Forerunner of Our Doubts

Few things are more terrifying than truly considering that something we have believed to be true might actually be false. Especially when it is a truth we have considered foundational—one that has directed our thoughts, words, actions, relationships, and decisions.

I'm stressing this because John's struggle wasn't his struggle alone. If the crisis of faith is not something *every* believer must undergo, it's certainly one that many will and do. Again, John was forerunning. Certainly, he was laying a path that Jesus's disciples would soon walk.

---

[2] An in-depth study of Jesus's apostolic commissioning can be read on my blog, in parts 138–158. For a complete index of posts see rachelstarrthomson.com/2016/07/08/gospel-of-matthew-series.

If we may jump ahead in the story a little, the triumphal entry was right around the corner—and immediately after that, the cleansing of the temple, Gethsemane, and Jesus's arrest, trial, and crucifixion.

Every follower of Jesus at that point would find themselves facing the same question John asked: *"Are you the One who is to come, or should we expect someone else?"*

With that question come many others, some intellectual, many personal. If you are not the One—where did we go wrong? How did we misread the Scriptures? Or is it the Scriptures that have failed? And personally—if you are not the One, have I wasted my life? Have I lost my closest relationships, turned down opportunities, and failed to pursue certain goals for nothing? In thinking I was doing right, have I been making a series of terrible mistakes all along?

Our questions range from the intimate and personal—*"maybe God doesn't love me"*—to the comprehensive (*"maybe God doesn't exist"*).

In the gospel of Matthew, "Are you the One" was about to become *the* question on everyone's minds.

For John in prison, doubt was real and pressing. He *needed* an answer. For the disciples only a year and a half later, it would be the same. They thought they understood their place in the storyline of history, but that storyline was about to take a massive plot twist with the potential to shatter their entire paradigm.

Jesus didn't really give John a straight answer—he just pointed him back to the Old Testament again. And the disciples had to wait three days for the resurrection to get their assurance that they hadn't "missed it" by following Jesus.

Our answers are, quite honestly, found in the same places: in the Scriptures and in the resurrection. And in some ways our crises of faith don't have the same urgency.

And yet they do.

Because when we come to such a moment of truth in our lives, so much depends on the answers.

A few years ago I got talking to someone at a business conference. He shared with me that he had been raised by missionary parents, but as a college student he had walked away from his childhood faith. I didn't know all the details of his journey, but—somewhat to my surprise—I found myself encouraging him in the path he had chosen. Sometimes in the church I think we are guilty of handing our children (or our new converts) a basketful of answers and telling them, "These are the answers. Now your job is to hold tightly to them and never, ever let go." The trouble is that if they have not experienced the freedom to discover their own questions and seek out the truth, the "answers" we give them will lack weight, and the recipients will have no personal ownership of them. Jesus, who said, "Ask, and it will be given to you; seek, and you will find; knock, and it will be opened to you,"[3] never betrayed a fear of questions. In fact, he invited seekers and had a way of taking them continually deeper in their questions and in the answers to be found.

---

3 Matthew 7:7, ESV

In the interaction laid out in Matthew 11:1–19, it's noteworthy that Jesus didn't rebuke John, or his disciples, for their question. Not in the least. He gave them an answer (of sorts), encouraged them to seek further, and went on to praise John to his disciples and all of their hearers. The implication is clear: *Jesus is okay with questions. God is big enough to handle our doubts, and even our complaints.* Doubts are not a problem to God, but he does prefer that we bring them to him, rather than keeping them quiet and letting them fester, or only talking about them to other people.

The best place to express doubt is prayer. The second best place to express it is in honest conversation with people of good hearts and open minds. Questions are best *asked*.

But if Jesus is okay with questions, we must also be okay with answers. What I mean by that is, for many of us, I believe doubt and disappointment come as a result of expecting Jesus to be someone other than who he is, and/or to be doing something other than what he's doing. The resolution of doubt may not be discovering that we were right all along, but rather, discovering that we were (at least in part) wrong—and that we are now being invited into a story that is bigger, or maybe just different, than what we thought. We then have a choice: accept the story we're being given, or cling to the old one as a basis for either doggedly hanging onto faith or rejecting it altogether.

If we ask questions, we have to accept that we may not *like* the answers. They may be unfamiliar, off-putting, or personally demanding in a way our old assumptions were not.

Asking questions means we will get answers. It doesn't guarantee anything about the nature of those answers. So going forth with our doubts, actually carrying them to Jesus in the open air, putting words to them, and requesting an answer, is an enterprise fraught with peril. We are accepting that peril by choosing to seek.

When people fall away from the faith, other people rush in with a multitude of answers for why that happens. We usually point to a lack. It was lack of apologetics. Lack of personal relationship. Lack of community. Lack of personal spirituality. Lack of roots. I don't think any one of these issues is sufficient in itself to explain why Christians leave the faith. They may *all* be valid and present to varying degrees. This book, therefore, isn't a book of apologetics or a book of answers at all, really. It's a story, one in which I think most of us can find ourselves. In the specifics of John's journey, we might recognize the universal shape of ours.

Before we go looking for specific answers, then, I think it's wise for us to understand John's questions more thoroughly—where they came from, what they meant, and how Jesus's answers changed the storyline John had thought he was living.

John's specific questions probably won't be the same as ours. But doubt is the same in every age and for everyone who experiences it. So my hope is that in his story, we will find companionship—and direction—for ours.

Chapter 2:
A Quick Interlude on the Nature of Faith

Faith does not exist in a vacuum. Not biblical faith, anyway.

In the catchphrasey way "faith" is frequently used these days, the word seems to mean a special feeling of belief or certainty, frequently without any basis in reality or reason. Like hope on steroids.

Without having read *The Secret*, I'll venture to say that many of us think of faith the same way true believers think of the Law of Attraction: it's something we summon up from within ourselves in order to influence God, or the Universe, to behave in accordance with our preferences. As Christians we may believe God wants us to summon up this faith when we approach him, so it's common in some circles to say we "have faith for" something or other—"faith for healing," "faith for breakthrough," "faith for my children to come back to the Lord," "faith for a good grade."

Faith as the Bible describes it, however, is not something we initiate or call up from within ourselves. Most basically, biblical faith is trust in God himself—that is, trust in God in the same sense that we trust in a person we consider trustworthy. Drilling down further, biblical faith *for* a specific thing is a response to something God *says* or *does*. That is, it's based on God's initiative and will as *he* chooses to express it. That being the case, it isn't "faith for" we need; it's "faith in."

Romans 10:16–17 states this clearly, and the rest of the New Testament clearly comes back to it. God, in his nature, words, and actions, is the basis of real faith. "Faith" that doesn't originate in what God says and whom he reveals himself to be is not really faith at all:

> So then faith comes by hearing, and hearing by the word of God.[1]

> [Abraham] did not waver in unbelief at God's promise but was strengthened in his faith and gave glory to God, because he was fully convinced that *what He had promised He was also able to perform.*[2]

> But if there is no resurrection of the dead, then Christ has not been raised; *and if Christ has not been raised, then our proclamation is without foundation, and so is your faith.*[3]

---

1 Romans 10:16–17, NKV
2 Romans 4:19–21, my emphasis
3 1 Corinthians 15:13–14. This theme runs throughout the Bible. To mention just a couple more: Colossians 2:12: "Having been buried with Him in baptism, you were also raised with Him through faith *in the working of God,* who raised Him from the dead." 1 Timothy 1:3–5: "Instruct certain people not to teach different doctrine or to pay attention to myths and endless genealogies. These promote empty speculations *rather than God's plan, which operates by faith.* Now the goal *of our instruction* is love that comes from a pure heart, a good conscience, *and a sincere faith.*" (All emphasis mine.)

THE CONTENT OF FAITH

Since faith requires God to have said or done something specific, it's not nebulous or self-generated. To put it another way: "faith" as it is described in the Bible, and as it has traditionally been understood throughout Christian history, has a specific content, and that content is drawn from the words of God and the person or actions of God. Hebrews 3:14 speaks of a faith grounded not in wishful thinking but in reality: "For we have become companions of the Messiah if we hold firmly until the end the reality that we had at the start."[4]

This concept will be more familiar to us if we come from a background grounded in creeds or liturgy. We might then think less in terms of "faith" as something personal and dynamic, and more in terms of *"the* faith"—something fixed and external to us. *The* faith can be understood as a set of doctrinal statements to which we give intellectual assent, along with a set of practices to which we commit ourselves. *The* faith, unlike faith as an inner energy of our own, existed before us and will still be here long after we are gone, and it arose entirely without our help.

Although we do need to receive this external "faith" into ourselves so it becomes personal and dynamic, this whole idea is closer to biblical faith than the wishful thinking espoused by popular culture (in and out of the church) today. But again, the key is that in order for

---

[4] The Greek word translated "reality" in the Holman Christian Standard Bible is often translated "confidence" or "assurance." The word connotes a solid foundation, substance, or underlying substructure—something *real* and therefore worthy of confidence.

anything to be worthy of *our* faith (in the sense of trust or believing), God must have originated it. And in most cases, it will begin with his speaking—his "word."[5] That's why it matters so deeply that "the Christian faith" be based on the Scriptures, the history they relate, and the revelation they offer, and not just on the traditions or reasoning of human beings.[6]

This shouldn't really be surprising. Within a Christian worldview, it's completely reasonable. After all, we believe that we live in a universe created by the speaking of God: "Then God said, 'Let there be light,' and there was light" … "By faith we understand that the universe was created by the word of God, so that what is seen was not made out of things that are visible."[7] God's words create; what he says, *is;* or if you prefer, what he says, becomes. God's Word defines and creates reality. At times we hear the speaking before we see the manifestation, but that doesn't mean we are putting our faith in something unreal; it just means God has given us reality in a latent form. Jesus frequently compared the kingdom of

---

5 In recent years the terms "word of God" and "Scripture" or "Bible" have become conflated, but while they overlap, they are not the same thing. The term "word of God," as it's used in the Scripture, means anything that God says. It includes his prophetic word, spoken directly or through messengers; the words he speaks to our hearts; and his promises. In a more mysterious sense, Jesus himself is the "Word of God" (John 1:1, 14). The word "Scripture" comes from the Latin root *scribere*, which means "to write": the Scriptures, therefore, are the *written* word of God. And the Bible (again from Latin, *biblia*, which means "books") is the collection of those writings.

6 This is also why it matters so much that the Scriptures actually be "inspired," as we have always claimed they are—that is, that they be the work of the Holy Spirit through human writers and not just the work of the human writers on their own.

7 Genesis 1:3; Hebrews 11:3, ESV

God, and the word of God that brings the kingdom, to seed: like an acorn that has fallen into the ground and begun to germinate, it is here, it real, it is alive, and it is changing things, but we do not yet see it in its fully grown form.

At the outset, this is both comforting and humbling. We live in a day and age when faith is so often spoken of in highly subjective, personal, and internalized terms that it's easy to forget we actually possess a heritage of *content*, a set of teachings, practices, and beliefs based on historical events—*a* faith. We may question this faith, but in doing so we aren't just questioning our own perceptions or assumptions, nor are we questioning a fad diet or a meme we saw on the Internet. We're questioning something that has been laid down over nearly three thousand years by some of the most intelligent and remarkable people who have ever lived. That doesn't mean it's right, of course, but it does mean it's not a flash in the pan. If you go beyond Christianity to the question of theism (belief in God) generally, the picture is even more stark.[8] Nearly every human being who has ever lived has

---

[8] As far as we know, atheists have always existed; but they have always constituted a tiny minority. In 2007, the *Encyclopedia Britannica* released an article entitled "Religion: Year in Review 2007," edited by Darrell J. Turner, with a table labeled "Worldwide Adherents of All Religions by Six Continental Areas, Mid-2007." They put the number of atheists of the world's entire population at 2%, with the number identifying as "nonreligious" at 11.7%. Not that it proves anything, but Christianity in its many iterations led the charge at 33.3% of the world's population—one in every three people. It's also interesting to note that at an estimated 128,048,000, the vast majority of modern-day atheists were located in Asia, suggesting that China—with its aggressively atheist government and enormous population—accounts for an outsized number of self-proclaimed nonbelievers today. Yet compared to China's total population in 2007 of 1.318 billion people,

believed in a god of some kind; nearly every human being living today still does.[9] Again, this doesn't make theism true, but it should make us humble in the way we approach our questions about it.

To return to the main point: in biblical thinking, faith is based on something external to us: in most cases, it's based on God's stated nature and intentions. If we believe something, even believe it *with all our hearts*, but it did not originate with God, then our belief is not biblical faith. It's little more than wishful thinking.

The roots of all kinds of crisis lie right here: that we have a tendency to try to put God's feet to the fire in ways that are not justified by his own words—to hold him to promises he hasn't made.

Resolving our doubts is not as simple as giving ourselves a slap on the wrist, though. We may have good theological reasons for believing we can claim certain

---

even this number is small; and that in a country where the state is officially atheist and religious adherents are routinely harassed or even repressed. See web.archive.org/web/20131212154920/http://www.britannica.com/EBchecked/topic/1360391/Religion-Year-In-Review-2007.

9 In the West, our perspective on this is unavoidably warped by our immediate surroundings. Most of us live in a "post-Christian" society, and while rumors of the death of Christianity have been grossly exaggerated (as Mark Twain might have said), we are confronted loudly and often with post-Christian, humanist, and even atheist ways of thinking. Not so most of the world. Nearly twenty years ago now, Philip Jenkins pointed out that the center of Christianity has moved south, such that the "typical Christian" is no longer a white Caucasian male but a Nigerian woman. While Christianity may be declining in Europe and North America, everywhere else in the world it is rapidly growing both in numbers and in influence. See Philip Jenkins, *The Next Christendom: The Coming of Global Christianity,* 3rd edition (New York: Oxford University Press, 2011).

promises. We may believe we have personally heard God speak to us. We may be reading a promise right off the page of the Bible, with its context and conditions recognized and accounted for, and yet we are still not seeing it fulfilled and we are still feeling disappointed and angry and offended and afraid or simply skeptical, or we are feeling just the glimmers of any of those things, and they are shaking our world.

It was that way for John, I think.

John had certain expectations of the Messiah, and of Jesus as the Messiah, and none of them came out of a vacuum. His expectations did not originate with himself. He knew the Scripture and he heard from the Spirit of God. He had faith, and he was committed to "the faith." In every possible respect, his faith was real and biblical in nature.

So what did John believe?

CHAPTER 3:
What John Believed: The Story of Israel and the One to Come

When John asked "Are you the One who is to come," it was clear he had a specific "One" in mind. From the Scriptures—from what God had said through the written law and prophets—he knew to expect a savior.

Growing up in Sunday school, I acquired a loose understanding of what the Jewish people might have expected such a "savior" to be like. I learned that in the time of Jesus, the people of Israel were waiting for God to send someone who would literally save them from their earthly troubles by freeing them from the Romans. I also gathered that this expected savior was called "the Messiah," and that "Messiah" was essentially New Testament-speak for "savior." As well, I picked up the information that "Christ" is just the Greek version of the Hebrew word "Messiah"—which is actually quite a helpful thing to know.

This loose grasp was not wrong, but the operative word is loose" To really understand John's questions, and therefore his doubts, it's helpful to understand with greater clarity where he got his expectations about the Messiah and why Jesus might have caused him to doubt—or at least qualify—them.

I should also note that back in Sunday school, I developed the assumption that the Old Testament *clearly* prophesied a heap of things that Christians believe about Jesus. For example, that the savior would be born of a virgin, that he would be the Son of God, and that he would die for the sins of the whole world; that he would be raised from the dead on the third day; and that he would save people primarily in a *spiritual* sense, atoning for their guilt and enabling them to live forever in heaven with him. Whether or not I was explicitly taught this, I picked up the notion that all these things were plain and obvious in the prophetic Scriptures and that Israel only missed them because their thinking was so worldly and earthbound—so essentially superficial and childish.

But while I would argue that all of the above is *present* in the Old Testament, none of those ideas about the Messiah are *obvious* there. If John expected none of those things, and plenty of worldly, earthbound deliverance by a human warrior-king, his expectations—and Jewish expectations overall—were far from superficial, childish, or lacking in biblical grounds.

The truth is this: when it came to the Messiah and the work he would do, the Old Testament was both remarkably clear and strong and remarkably, well, unclear and mysterious. In fact, it was very possible to read the Old Testament Scriptures and come away believing that

God would act in the future to deliver his people, but not through a human agent—a "Messiah"—at all.

So what *is* clear from the Old Testament, and how did the Jews arrive at their expectation of a human savior? Why did the term "Messiah" (or Christ) end up applied to this "One who is to come," so much so that the great question of the gospels—and certainly of the gospel of Matthew from chapter 11 onward—is "Are you the Messiah, or should we expect someone else?"[1]

And finally, what does all this have to do with the Christian ideas about Jesus, especially of Jesus as the Son of God and the spiritual savior of the world?

"I Set Before You Blessing and Curse"

Before we can really understand what God's promise of a savior was all about, we have to understand the Bible's wider context for that promise—and to do that, we need to see the story of Scripture as it unfolded in the thousand years before Jesus came.

Just a word before we go on: At this point in our conversation about doubt, we are going to embark on a fairly long journey together. In fact, our walk through the Old Testament narrative will take up roughly half

---

1 Matthew, writing twenty to fifty years after Jesus's resurrection, gives the game away. Speaking of John in prison, he says, "When John heard in prison what *the Messiah* was doing, he sent a message by his disciples ..." (Matthew 11:2, my emphasis). So long after the fact, Matthew considered it obvious that Jesus *was* the Messiah. This is why he and the other gospel writers persistently refer to Jesus as "Jesus Christ," or "Jesus the Messiah." But at the time these events were unfolding, it wasn't obvious, and Jesus hadn't yet declared himself openly.

this book. But it isn't a detour. Remember, our faith, like John's, has a content—and the story of Scripture gives us that content. If we want to better understand our own struggles and doubts, it helps to understand the story we're living. As the pieces come together, we may even find ourselves suddenly seeing the landscape around us differently, as the Bible offers us a map for our hopes and our fears and helps us figure out where we're standing right now.

With that introduction, then, let's continue.

Although it's easy to get lost in some of the details, the Old Testament ultimately tells one great, sweeping story. We might call this "the story of Israel and God." In Genesis, the first book of the Bible, we read about creation and the fall of man. We then see God and man struggling against each other for a time, until God chooses a man named Abram (later "Abraham") and covenants with him. The covenant is eternal and unilateral (or one-sided) in its formal structure,[2] and it revolves around the promise of blessing:

The Lord[3] said to Abram:

---

[2] In the Genesis 12 version of the Abrahamic covenant, God says "I will" six times, but there is no corresponding "if you will" or condition attached. This is in contrast to the later Mosaic covenant, which includes many conditions binding on the people in order for the promised blessings to come about.

[3] In English Bibles, the word "Lord" written all in capitals indicates the underlying Hebrew word is *YHWH*, the proper name of God as revealed to Moses and commonly transliterated "Yahweh" or "Jehovah." (The correct pronunciation of the word has been lost.) When *Lord* is used in the Old Testament using standard lowercase letters, the word underlying it is *Adonai*, an honoring title meaning "lord" or "ruler." This English usage mirrors Jewish tradition. Out of concern for properly reverencing the name of God, and avoiding the sin

> Go out from your land,
> your relatives,
> and your father's house
> to the land that I will show you.
> I will make you into a great nation,
> I will bless you,
> I will make your name great,
> and you will be a blessing.
> I will bless those who bless you,
> I will curse those who treat you with contempt,
> and all the peoples on earth
> will be blessed through you.[4]

The Hebrew concept of *blessing* revolves around the idea of life and fruitfulness. It connotes prosperity and health, peace, freedom from trouble, and victory over one's enemies. It is the opposite of *cursing*, which withers and makes barren, bringing trouble and evil with it.

Abram was seventy-five years old when God made this initial promise to him. About ten years later, God appeared to him again. Abram, now eighty-five years old and still childless, complained to the Lord that the promise to him of fathering a great nation was growing increasingly unlikely to be fulfilled and that a servant would become his heir. At this point, God formalized the

---

of "taking the name of YHWH in vain," devout Jews when reading the Scriptures would not pronounce the name of God. Instead they would say *Adonai*, "Lord"; or *Adoshem*, "Lord of the Name," when they encountered the word YHWH in the text. Today, *Adonai* is still used in liturgical contexts, while *Hashem* ("the Name") is the more common way of referring to God outside of such contexts. Since the personal name of God is more intimate and personally revealing than the honorific *Lord*, I find it helpful to distinguish them in my own reading and know what underlying word I'm looking at.

4 Genesis 12:1–3

covenant with Abram through a ritual sacrifice and added three very specific promises: Abram's heir would be a child of his own body, his descendants would be greatly numerous, and his descendants would inherit a specific swath of land to dwell in:

> Now the word of the Lord came to him: "This one will not be your heir; instead, one who comes from your own body will be your heir." He took him outside and said, "Look at the sky and count the stars, if you are able to count them." Then He said to him, "Your offspring will be that numerous."
>
> Abram believed the Lord, and He credited it to him as righteousness.
>
> He also said to him, "I am Yahweh who brought you from Ur of the Chaldeans to give you this land to possess."
>
> But he said, "Lord God, how can I know that I will possess it?"
>
> He said to him, "Bring Me a three-year-old cow, a three-year-old female goat, a three-year-old ram, a turtledove, and a young pigeon."
>
> So he brought all these to Him, split them down the middle, and laid the pieces opposite each other, but he did not cut up the birds. Birds of prey came down on the carcasses, but Abram drove them away …
>
> When the sun had set and it was dark, a smoking fire pot and a flaming torch appeared and passed between the divided animals. On that day the Lord

made a covenant with Abram, saying, "I give this land to your offspring, from the brook of Egypt to the Euphrates River ..."[5]

Abraham's descendants through his son Isaac inherited this covenant, but in order to remain within its covering and continue moving toward its ultimate goal—the blessing of "all peoples of the earth" through them—they needed to *practice* righteousness and faith in God. After all, as James would bluntly declare many years later, "faith without works is dead."[6] Unless they had a way of putting their beliefs about God and their own special calling into concrete action in the real world, the people of Israel would not continue in relationship with God.

If you like, they needed a program of spiritual formation. And this is where the Mosaic Law entered the picture.

REMAINING IN GOD'S LOVE

At this point, Christians often start talking about legalism and "the curse of the law," as though the law itself was a curse, overburdening the Israelites with a moral weight they could not possibly carry and essentially tricking them into becoming guilty of sin. But this is a misreading of the Scripture. Paul was clear about *why* the law was given, and it wasn't to curse the people or overload them with a burden of legalism. The law was intended to keep them safe—to watch over them as a guardian until the goal of the covenant could be reached.

---

5 Genesis 15:4–11, 17–20
6 James 2:26

> Why then was the law given? It was added because of transgressions until the Seed to whom the promise was made would come ... The law, then, was our guardian until Christ, so that we could be justified by faith. But since that faith has come, we are no longer under a guardian, for you are all sons of God through faith in Christ Jesus.[7]

In one of his most famous parables, Jesus told the story of a man with two sons. The younger son demanded his inheritance, left his father's house, and spent the money in reckless living. Reduced to poverty and humiliation, the younger son decided to go home and ask for a servant's job in his father's house. But in an unexpected and beautiful turn, the father had been watching for him. When he saw his son on the horizon, he ran to him, embraced him, kissed him, soaked his tunic with his tears, and declared that his son who was lost had been found; his son who was dead had come to life again. It was the kind of welcome and reception we all dream of, and Jesus claimed it was the heart of God for every one of us.

I think the story demonstrates something about the nature of obedience as it relates to God's love (and to the law, which is why I mention it here). In John 15:9–10, Jesus said:

> As the Father has loved Me, I have also loved you. Remain in My love. If you keep My commands you will remain in My love, just as I have kept My Father's commands and remain in His love.

---

[7] Galatians 3:19, 24–26

The implication here *isn't* that God is a legalist and his love depends on our behavior. Like the father in the story of the prodigal son, God's love never changes. When we fail to remain in his love, that doesn't mean his love for us ceases to exist. *It means that we remove ourselves from its reach.* The prodigal son was always the object of his father's devoted love. His father's resources were always there for him. But to receive them, to experience them, he had to come back home. He had to choose to remain in his father's love.

The Mosaic Law was calculated to do the same thing: to keep the people of Israel at home in the love of God. Again, it gave them a concrete way to express and embody their faith, to practice their covenant love for God in the real world and to receive his expressions of covenant love for them. In Romans 11, Paul compared the situation of the Israelites under the law to that of a "cultivated olive tree," brought up in "the kindness of God" and needing to remain in it—in contrast to the Gentiles, who were like a "wild olive tree."[8] The law was not a prison or a curse; it was a greenhouse.

The Mosaic law, however, was qualitatively different from the earlier covenant with Abraham. The law was also covenantal, but unlike the Abrahamic covenant, it wasn't one-sided, with everything depending solely on the action of God to accomplish. It was a mutual covenant that required things of the people just as it required things of God. The people could choose whether to remain in it and meet their obligations, but if they did not, there would be consequences.

---

8 Romans 11:13–24, especially verses 17 and 22.

And again, the central issue was blessing:

> See, today I have set before you life and prosperity, death and adversity. For I am commanding you today to love the Lord your God, to walk in His ways, and to keep His commands, statutes, and ordinances, so that you may live and multiply, *and the Lord your God may bless you in the land you are entering to possess*. But if your heart turns away and you do not listen and you are led astray to bow down to other gods and worship them, I tell you today that you will certainly perish and will not live long in the land you are entering to possess across the Jordan.
>
> *I call heaven and earth as witnesses against you today that I have set before you life and death, blessing and curse.* Choose life so that you and your descendants may live, love the Lord your God, obey Him, and remain faithful to Him. For He is your life, and He will prolong your life in the land the Lord swore to give to your fathers Abraham, Isaac, and Jacob.[9]

In his love, God had promised Abraham that he would bless his descendants—and through them, the entire world.[10] But Abraham's descendants continued to struggle against God just as humanity before them had done. So God gave them the law to keep them in the

---

[9] Deuteronomy 30:15–20, my emphasis

[10] In Scripture, love is the only reason given for the Lord's choice of Abraham (and beyond him, for his desire to bless the world through Abraham). "The LORD was devoted to you and chose you, not because you were more numerous than all peoples, for you were the fewest of all peoples. But because the LORD loved you and kept the oath He swore to your fathers, He brought you out with a strong hand and redeemed you from the place of slavery" (Deuteronomy 7:7–8).

greenhouse, so to speak—to ensure that they "remained in his love" until the time came to fulfill all his promises to Abraham.

The Mosaic Law, however, had a necessary negative side. Just as *shalom* (total well-being) could rightly be called "the blessing of the law," so a whole host of negative consequences were attached to the law as its "curse."[11] This is what Paul means when he talks about the "curse of the law."[12] The law itself was never a curse; it was a good gift from a good God looking to keep his children safe at home, under his protection and in ongoing relationship with him. But the law did *contain* a curse: a promise of destruction if the people chose to engage in unrighteousness and break faith with God.[13,14]

---

11 The list of curses is found in Deuteronomy 28, as is the list of blessings that accompany faithfulness to the law. Taken as a whole, these curses comprise "the curse."
12 Galatians 3:13
13 The English phrase "break faith" provides insight into another aspect of biblical faith: the idea of "faithfulness." The Greek word we translate "faith," "belief," and "trust"—*pistis*—is also translated "faithfulness." A trust-relationship goes two ways, so to "keep faith" with someone is to be faithful toward them, while to "break faith" is to be unfaithful. This nuance means it is quite proper to describe biblical faith as being fundamentally about relationship and allegiance, even more than it is about intellectual assent to a given set of propositions.
14 It's often asserted within the church that the law was innately impossible to keep, making every act of sin a breaking of covenant and placing everyone under the law's curse. What's overlooked is that the law itself contained provisions for atonement and forgiveness. The law had built-in room for human messiness and a way to be reconciled to God. What brought the nation under the curse was not individual failures to keep the law perfectly but national failure to be reconciled to God. The curse came because the nation turned its back on the law, rejected the covenant, and chose to follow and worship idols instead of Yahweh.

This, I should point out, was a common feature of two-way covenants, and in fact even today it makes sense. When you make a significant commitment and voluntarily take on obligations, consequences follow on breaking that commitment and failing to meet those obligations. How much more so when the covenant-breaking actions in themselves were, for the most part, dehumanizing and evil in nature? Since the law was a *moral* law given to Israel by the One tasked with justly judging all of humanity, breaking the law typically involved immoral actions that carried severe natural consequences and called out for judgment. *Your brother's blood calls out to me from the ground,* God told Cain after the murder of his brother Abel. In injustice, blood still calls out. Among the covenant-breaking behaviors most strongly condemned by the prophets were treachery and betrayal, kidnapping and slavery, adultery, theft and cheating, and the oppression of the poor and of ethnic minorities by those in power. It's ironic that people antagonistic to the idea of God commonly object to his being a God of "judgment, anger, and wrath"—while simultaneously complaining that if God really was powerful and good, he would do something about all the injustice in the world. We can't have it both ways.

God was not unfair to give Israel a covenant that contained harsh sanctions if they broke it. The very nature of breaking this particular covenant would demand sanctions if God were to be just. The key issue of covenant was faithfulness to God—that is, undivided allegiance to Yahweh as god, without worship of idols. But because God's covenant with Israel was mostly framed in moral terms, and because he is a God of righteousness and justice, breaking the covenant also resulted in heavy injustice in human terms.

In any case, what is clear from the record of the Bible is that Israel *did* break faith with God—early and often. With the law clearly judging their actions and pronouncing curses on them, the people engaged in blatant idolatry and all kinds of evil. Despite the fact that they were clearly "outside of the greenhouse" at this point, and that as a nation they had agreed to be judged by the law,[15] God demonstrated patience for hundreds of years, withholding large-scale judgment and sending prophets to call Israel back to faithfulness.

As a result, the days of Moses were followed by about four hundred years of fits and starts—predictable waves in which the people rejected the law and turned to idols; God sent a small-scale judgment on them along with a prophet calling them to repentance and covenant renewal; the people turned back to God; God prospered them with the promised blessings of the law; and the people rejected the law and turned to idols again.

One gets the sense of a prodigal son who, two months after coming home to a warm welcome, demands still more of his inheritance and takes off to waste it again—over and over. But God had long ago declared himself to be compassionate and longsuffering, and so he was.

The Lord came down in a cloud, stood with [Moses] there, and proclaimed His name Yahweh. Then the Lord passed in front of him and proclaimed:

---
[15] See Exodus 24:1–7

> Yahweh—Yahweh is a compassionate and gracious God, slow to anger and rich in faithful love and truth, maintaining faithful love to a thousand generations, forgiving wrongdoing, rebellion, and sin. But He will not leave the guilty unpunished, bringing the consequences of the fathers' wrongdoing on the children and grandchildren to the third and fourth generation.[16]

Because of God's faithfulness both to Abraham and to the people of Israel, he eventually brought them to the apex of their glory as a nation during the reigns of David and Solomon even though they had never been fully faithful to him. This was very much the Golden Age of Israel, characterized by the presence of God in their midst via the temple, by victory over their enemies, by prosperity, and by peace.

In fact, the Scriptures consciously highlight the fulfillment of *every* blessing promised to Abraham and Moses during this period.[17] As far as the writers of the Old Testament were concerned, God had kept all his promises. In speaking of Solomon's reign, the writer of 1 Kings consciously draws on the language of Abrahamic promise:

> Judah and Israel *were as numerous as the sand by the sea;* they were eating, drinking, and rejoicing. Solomon ruled over all the kingdoms *from the Euphrates River to the land of the Philistines and as*

---

16 Exodus 34:5–7
17 I have Steve Atkerson of New Testament Reformation Fellowship to thank for this insight, in his 2009 sermon "Comparing New Covenant Theology, Covenant Theology & Dispensational Theology." As of October 11, 2019, a PDF with notes can be accessed at sermonaudio.com/sermoninfo.asp?SID=105121950353.

> *far as the border of Egypt.* They offered tribute and served Solomon all the days of his life ... he had dominion over everything west of the Euphrates from Tiphsah to Gaza and over all the kings west of the Euphrates. He had peace on all his surrounding borders. Throughout Solomon's reign, Judah and Israel lived in safety from Dan to Beer-sheba, each man under his own vine and his own fig tree ...
>
> God gave Solomon wisdom, very great insight, and understanding as vast as the sand on the seashore. Solomon's wisdom was greater than the wisdom of all the people of the East, greater than all the wisdom of Egypt ... *His reputation extended to all the surrounding nations ... People came from everywhere, sent by every king on earth who had heard of his wisdom, to listen to Solomon's wisdom.*[18]

The language to Abraham of "stars of the sky and the sand of the sea" was always hyperbolic, probably not intended to be taken literally, and again, the words used in Kings and Chronicles suggests their inspired writers considered the promise fulfilled. As God had promised, the borders of Israel stretched from the Euphrates to the Nile. Even the promise of "blessing the nations through you" is seen in the Golden Age: it's the reason 1 Kings 4 speaks of the nations coming to hear Solomon's wisdom, as personified by the queen of Sheba in 1 Kings 10 and 2 Chronicles 9. In expanding on the Abrahamic promise, Moses had added the promises of victory over their enemies, peace, and material prosperity, details that are likewise consciously underscored in 1 Kings 4 to demonstrate that the Golden Age of David and Solomon had

---

18 1 Kings 4:20–21, 24–25, 29–30, 31, 34; all emphasis mine.

brought about the fulfilment of every covenant promise. Most of all, the building of the temple as a permanent dwelling place for Yahweh in the midst of his people signified the fullness of God's blessing on them.

The Golden Age, though, was tragically short-lived. Although David was a deeply flawed human being, he nevertheless remained faithful to God all his life. He sinned and fell outrageously, but he humbled himself and came back to God seeking forgiveness and cleansing—which he certainly received. But cracks appeared in the foundation of David's house as a consequence of his sins, and several of his sons engaged in violent and rebellious behaviors in a bid for the throne that nearly split the nation. Finally Solomon, God's chosen among David's sons, ascended the throne. But unlike David, Solomon followed in the pattern of his unfaithful ancestors by embracing the worship of idols and rejecting the covenant. In one of the Old Testament's most tragic ironies, the same king who built the temple for God's presence also led the nation into profaning that presence through their worship of idols.

At this point, the story of Israel's downfall begins. Once again there is a pattern of rejecting God and then turning back to him, but the overall trajectory is downward. Now when God sent prophets, they were not calling Israel to repent in order to turn away small-scale judgments. They were warning of tremendous judgment to come—of a day not far in the future when the curse of the law would come fully into play, the nation would be dissolved, and the people would be sent into exile among enemy nations.

Again, it's important to remember that God continued to give his people time and the chance to turn things around. Even with this path of destruction clearly in view, he sent prophets to give the people opportunity to repent and renew their covenant with him—and he did this not for a few months or a year or two, but for another three hundred years and more.

God's patience was so far-reaching, in fact, that many people assumed it meant he wasn't really involved at all, or that he was powerless to do anything about injustice. So the psalmists and prophets frequently complained:

> Lord, God of vengeance—
> God of vengeance, appear.
> Rise up, Judge of the earth;
> repay the proud what they deserve.
> Lord, how long will the wicked—
> how long will the wicked gloat?
> They pour out arrogant words;
> all the evildoers boast.
> Lord, they crush Your people;
> they afflict Your heritage.
> They kill the widow and the foreigner
> and murder the fatherless.
> They say, "The Lord doesn't see it.
> The God of Jacob doesn't pay attention."
> Pay attention, you stupid people!
> Fools, when will you be wise?
> Can the One who shaped the ear not hear,
> the One who formed the eye not see?
> The One who instructs nations,
> the One who teaches man knowledge—
> does He not discipline?[19]

---

19 Psalm 94:1–10

As God continually warned Israel through the prophets, however, the big judgment *was* coming. And it did. It came in two waves: first with the carrying away of the Northern Kingdom to Assyria in 722 BC, and then with the carrying away into exile of the Southern Kingdom to Babylon in 586 BC. God's time frames were long, but he kept his word—for good and for ill.

THE RULE OF THE CURSE— AND THE NEW PROMISES OF GOD

With the going of the exiles into Babylon, the era of the curse had begun. Remember, as we saw earlier, *from the standpoint of the Israelite historians, God did not owe his people anything more.* He had kept all his promises, even blessing the nation of Israel when he had good reasons not to do so. He had been generous and liberal in his interpretation of their faithfulness, and when their sins and unfaithfulness were too blatant to ignore, he had waited nearly half a millennium before bringing judgment on them—and that while giving loud and repeated opportunity for them to avert it completely.

It was, therefore, perfectly feasible that the story of Israel was simply over. They had covenanted with God, they had failed to keep the covenant, and he had discharged his responsibilities toward them and then said good-bye forever. The divorce was final and God, the wronged husband, didn't owe a penny of alimony.

Except that's not how it happened. God, who had kept all of his old promises, took the opportunity of judgment to make a whole long list of new ones.

"Look, the days are coming"—this is the Lord's declaration—"when I will make a new covenant with the house of Israel and with the house of Judah. This one will not be like the covenant I made with their ancestors when I took them by the hand to bring them out of the land of Egypt—a covenant they broke even though I had married them"—the Lord's declaration. "Instead, this is the covenant I will make with the house of Israel after those days"—the Lord's declaration. "I will put My teaching within them and write it on their hearts. I will be their God, and they will be My people. No longer will one teach his neighbor or his brother, saying, 'Know the Lord,' for they will all know Me, from the least to the greatest of them"—this is the Lord's declaration. "For I will forgive their wrongdoing and never again remember their sin."

> This is what the Lord says:
> The One who gives the sun for light by day,
> the fixed order of moon and stars for light by night,
> who stirs up the sea and makes its waves roar—
> Yahweh of Hosts is His name:
> If this fixed order departs from My presence—
> this is the Lord's declaration—
> then also Israel's descendants will cease
> to be a nation before Me forever.
> This is what the Lord says:
> If the heavens above can be measured
> and the foundations of the earth below explored,
> I will reject all of Israel's descendants
> because of all they have done—
> this is the Lord's declaration.[20]

---

[20] Jeremiah 31:31-37

There are two ways of looking at God's motivation to renew his covenant with Israel. One is simply to recognize that he was motivated by love. This was the reason explicitly given through Isaiah:

> Zion says, "The Lord has abandoned me;
> The Lord has forgotten me!"
> "Can a woman forget her nursing child,
> or lack compassion for the child of her womb?
> Even if these forget,
> yet I will not forget you.
> Look, I have inscribed you on the palms of My hands;
> your walls are continually before Me.[21]

But we can also gather a more implicit reason: although God had technically fulfilled his promises to Israel, the underlying *purpose* of those promises had not yet come to pass in its fullness. That purpose was blessing, shalom for the world. God had promised to bless the nations through Abraham, to multiply his descendants, give them an inheritance, and bring forth kings from his line. In all of these promises, we can discern a thread that goes back all the way to Adam in the garden of Eden, who was commanded to be fruitful and multiply, to inherit the earth, and to rule it as the image of God.[22] It's not too much of a stretch to realize that in choosing Abraham and his descendants, God's purpose involved the restoration of the human race—of the Eden we lost so long ago.[23]

---

[21] Isaiah 49:14–16
[22] Genesis 1:27–28.
[23] For more on this, see G.K. Beale, *A New Testament Biblical Theology* (Grand Rapids: Baker Academic, 2011).

Out of his love for his people *and* his commitment to seeing his own plan to completion, then, God declared that the story was not over. Jeremiah was not alone in announcing that God would do a glorious new work of covenanting, sanctifying, and restoring on the heels of judgment. Isaiah, Ezekiel, Hosea, Malachi, Micah, Zechariah, Zephaniah—prophet after prophet, in age after age—told the same story. After Israel's unfaithfulness had brought about its ultimate consequence, God would renew his promises to Abraham and continue to fulfill them in even greater measure. Moreover, he would take his divorced wife back again. The old Mosaic covenant was in shreds, so it wouldn't be used anymore; instead, he would make a new one.[24] The judgment that had come upon them would *not* be total, and he would not abandon them in the midst of it. Rather than good-bye and good riddance, God's presence would accompany his people into exile, and he would bless and prosper them in the land of their enemies *even during the rule and reign of the curse.*

Moreover, God promised, the Golden Age would come again. God had made a separate covenant with the family of David, and despite their horrific apostasy, he intended to keep it. A son of David would sit on the throne again. Like David, he would be a warrior-king who would free the people from their enemies. And like

---

[24] This is how I understand the promises regarding the new covenant, and I believe Jesus and the New Testament writers understood them this way as well—that it was to be a completely different covenant, replacing the old one. However, many of the Jews understood the promise as meaning the old, Mosaic covenant would be renewed; and many people today still understand these passages in that sense.

Solomon, he would be a king of peace, ushering in an era of incomparable prosperity, healing, and peace.

The Return of the King

Among the Old Testament books of prophecy, none quite compares to Isaiah. Sometimes called the prince of prophets, Isaiah functioned as the chief prophetic voice in the southern kingdom of Judah during the reigns of Uzziah (a decent king), Hezekiah (a righteous one), and Manasseh (probably the worst of all the southern kings, who practiced child sacrifice and is traditionally believed to have ordered Isaiah's death by sawing in half).

Approximately one hundred years before Babylon carried the princes and people of Judah away into exile, Isaiah prophesied Babylon's rise as an empire, the judgment of God that would come upon apostate Israel through it, the return of the exiles to the land, and ultimately, the incredible restoration to come in the distant future. Although Israel had gone into exile for their sins, God said, one day he would redeem them from the power of sin, the curse of the law, and their human enemies, bringing them out of captivity in Babylon just as he had brought their forefathers out of captivity to Egypt centuries earlier. And when that happened, God himself would come to dwell gloriously in their midst and establish his own kingdom among them. Since God had withdrawn his presence from the temple during the exile, the prophets speak of this future coming as a "return."

In chapters 40–55 of Isaiah, God describes this glorious return, climaxing in Isaiah 52 with the proclamation that "God reigns"—that is, God's kingdom has come:[25]

> "Wake up, wake up;
> put on your strength, Zion!
> Put on your beautiful garments,
> Jerusalem, the Holy City!
> For the uncircumcised and the unclean
> will no longer enter you.
> Stand up, shake the dust off yourself!
> Take your seat, Jerusalem.
> Remove the bonds from your neck,
> captive Daughter Zion."
> For this is what the Lord says:
> "You were sold for nothing,
> and you will be redeemed without silver."
> For this is what the Lord God says:
> "At first My people went down to Egypt to live there,
> then Assyria oppressed them without cause.
> So now what have I here"—
> this is the Lord's declaration—
> "that My people are taken away for nothing?
> Its rulers wail"—
> this is the Lord's declaration—
> "and My name is continually blasphemed all day long.
> Therefore My people will know My name;
> therefore they will know on that day
> that I am He who says:
> Here I am."
> How beautiful on the mountains

---

[25] N.T. Wright and Michael F. Bird, *The New Testament in Its World: An Introduction to the History, Literature, and Theology of the First Christians* (Grand Rapids: Zondervan Academic, 2019), 234–235

> are the feet of the herald,
> who proclaims peace,
> who brings news of good things,
> who proclaims salvation,
> who says to Zion, *"Your God reigns!"*
> The voices of your watchmen—
> they lift up their voices,
> shouting for joy together;
> for every eye will see
> *when the Lord returns to Zion.*[26]

Other prophets also emphasized these themes of redemption and deliverance, the return of God to dwell with his people, and the establishment of God's kingdom on the earth. Using an image of resurrection to represent this future day when God would dramatically act, Ezekiel wrote:

> This is what the Lord God says: "I am going to open your graves and bring you up from them, My people, and lead you into the land of Israel. You will know that I am Yahweh, My people, when I open your graves and bring you up from them. I will put My Spirit in you, and you will live, and I will settle you in your own land. Then you will know that I am Yahweh. I have spoken, and I will do it." This is the declaration of the Lord.
>
> "I will make a covenant of peace with them; it will be an everlasting covenant with them. I will establish and multiply them and will set My sanctuary among them forever. My dwelling place will be with them; I will be their God, and they will be My people."[27]

---

26 Isaiah 52:1–8, my emphasis.
27 Ezekiel 37:12–14, 26–27

Zephaniah wrote about this era of deliverance with special emphasis on God's kingship and presence. Like Isaiah, Ezekiel, and Jeremiah, he also connected this new era of redemption to the forgiveness of Israel's sins and their freedom, at long last, from the curse:

> Sing for joy, Daughter Zion;
> shout loudly, Israel!
> Be glad and rejoice with all your heart,
> Daughter Jerusalem!
> The Lord has removed your punishment;
> He has turned back your enemy.
> The King of Israel, Yahweh, is among you;
> you need no longer fear harm.
> On that day it will be said to Jerusalem:
> "Do not fear;
> Zion, do not let your hands grow weak.
> Yahweh your God is among you,
> a warrior who saves.
> He will rejoice over you with gladness.
> He will bring you quietness with His love.
> He will delight in you with shouts of joy."[28]

All of these prophets also made it clear that when God did all of this—forgiving his people, redeeming them from captivity, delivering them from their enemies, restoring them to their land, and making a new covenant with them in which he would come to dwell among them and reign as king—it would mean the beginning of a new age. This age would be an unprecedented era of peace, prosperity, and favor. Its impact would be so wide-reaching that it would affect more than Isra-

---

[28] Zephaniah 3:14–17

el: it would draw the nations of the world to Israel's God. As some commentators have pointed out, the idea of a "Messiah" was not entirely clear in the Hebrew Scriptures, but there was no question that God had promised a "Messianic age."[29]

> The prophet Micah described this coming era well:
> In the last days
> the mountain of the Lord's house
> will be established
> at the top of the mountains
> and will be raised above the hills.
> Peoples will stream to it,
> and many nations will come and say,
> "Come, let us go up to the mountain of the Lord,
> to the house of the God of Jacob.
> He will teach us about His ways
> so we may walk in His paths."
> For instruction will go out of Zion
> and the word of the Lord from Jerusalem.
> He will settle disputes among many peoples
> and provide arbitration for strong nations
> that are far away.
> They will beat their swords into plows,
> and their spears into pruning knives.
> Nation will not take up the sword against nation,
> and they will never again train for war.
> But each man will sit under his grapevine
> and under his fig tree
> with no one to frighten him.
> For the mouth of the Lord of Hosts
> has promised this.

---

29 See "Messianism: Jewish Messianism," *Encyclopedia of Religion* (Thomson Gale, 2005). Hosted at Encyclopedia.com.

> On that day—
> this is the Lord's declaration—
> I will assemble the lame
> and gather the scattered,
> those I have injured.
> I will make the lame into a remnant,
> those far removed into a strong nation.
> Then the Lord will rule over them in Mount Zion
> from this time on and forever.
> And you, watchtower for the flock,
> fortified hill of Daughter Zion,
> the former rule will come to you,
> sovereignty will come to Daughter Jerusalem.[30]

In this passage from Micah, as in Zephaniah 3 and Isaiah 52, it is *God* who will one day reign in Israel. The King whose return is so desperately needed isn't a human king at all, but Yahweh, the Lord of Hosts.

From our vantage point so many years later, it's important to remember that the Jewish people might have expected a human savior to come along at some point, but mostly, they expected God to act on their behalf just as he had when they came out of Egypt.

It was, after all, God they had sinned against. Only God could release them from their sins and truly bring them home again.

In a passage heavy with allusions to the exodus from Egypt, Isaiah wrote:

> This is what the Lord says—
> who makes a way in the sea,
> and a path through surging waters,

---

[30] Micah 4:1–4, 6–8

> who brings out the chariot and horse,
> the army and the mighty one together
> (they lie down, they do not rise again;
> they are extinguished, quenched like a wick)—
> "Do not remember the past events,
> pay no attention to things of old.
> Look, I am about to do something new;
> even now it is coming. Do you not see it?
> Indeed, I will make a way in the wilderness,
> rivers in the desert.
> The animals of the field will honor Me,
> jackals and ostriches,
> because I provide water in the wilderness,
> and rivers in the desert,
> to give drink to My chosen people.
> The people I formed for Myself
> will declare My praise ...
> It is I who sweep away your transgressions
> for My own sake
> and remember your sins no more."[31]

ENTER THE MESSIAH

As we have seen, the primary emphasis of all these prophecies is the action, presence, and reign of God as *God's* kingdom came to Israel. Yet, some ancient prophecies also clearly pointed to *a person* who would take center stage as the kingdom of God was being established. This person would be an anointed king—a "Messiah." He would be a figure both priestly and kingly, and as we will see, he would come from the house of David.

The term *Messiah* (*Mashiach* in Hebrew) means

---
31 Isaiah 43:1–21, 25

"Anointed One." It comes from the Hebrew word *mashach*, which means to smear or anoint with oil. It implies a special consecration by God and God's appointment to a significant task. Specifically, anointing with oil was the ancient practice used to signify that someone was being consecrated as a king, priest, or prophet. Samuel anointed David as king long before he actually took the throne. Moses anointed his brother Aaron and his family, the Levites, to serve as Yahweh's priests. Elijah anointed Elisha to follow in his footsteps as prophet to Israel in one of its darkest hours. Occasionally objects were also anointed to make them holy to the Lord: the tabernacle, the ark of the covenant, the altar, the vessels used in the temple for service to God, the offerings given to God, and the daily shewbread were all anointed with oil.[32]

Originally, the Messiah wasn't necessarily expected to *cause* the era of deliverance and redemption—rather, many felt that his coming would be a sign that God had done as he promised and the Messianic Age had truly arrived.[33] But either way, Israel's hopes soon began to revolve around this human figure and the new age he would signify. As generations of Israelite teachers studied the Scriptures, their hopes for the future crystalized in the person of the Messiah. And slowly, he began to be seen not just as a sign of the new age but as a holy warrior king who would overthrow Israel's oppressors, resume the rule of David's family in Jerusalem, and *cause*

---

32 See Exodus 30–40 and Leviticus 2 and 8.
33 See "Messianism: Jewish Messianism," *Encyclopedia of Religion* (Thomson Gale, 2005). Hosted at Encyclopedia.com.

the new age to come in. He would be its active agent, the one who brought this earthly salvation about. Of course, he would not personally release the people of Israel from the curse or forgive their sins. *Only God could do that.* But once God had done that, the Messiah would arise to bring "salvation"—deliverance from Israel's enemies, and with it, the rule of the kingdom of God.

On this front, what I learned in Sunday school was right. In John the Baptist's time, the Messiah was not expected to be a "spiritual deliverer" or "personal savior" in the way we understand those terms today, but as a king who would overthrow the oppressive Roman regime, renew or exemplify devotion to the Mosaic law, and begin a reign of peace. By doing this, he would be a sign of God's renewed covenant and active presence among the people of Israel. The return of Yahweh and the rule of David would go together.

But the Old Testament does not predict the coming of "a Messiah" in the straightforward way I assumed it must when I was a child. It certainly doesn't predict the coming of a Messiah who clearly possesses the supernatural attributes we associate with Jesus. Those who studied the prophets didn't come away expecting a virgin birth, miracles, resurrection, or the second person of the Trinity. In other words, they didn't expect Yahweh incarnate. What they *did* expect was a king whose kingdom would be a human expression of God's kingdom. Specifically, they expected a son of David.

Chapter 4:
What John Believed: Messiah, Son of David

Earlier, we saw that the reigns of David and his son Solomon constituted Israel's Golden Age, when God fulfilled his original promises to the nation. It was an era of almost unbelievable victory, peace, prosperity, and international prominence for Israel. It was also the era when God came to dwell in the temple in Jerusalem, centering the worship of God in the Holy City and making his presence permanent there. Spiritually and materially, there had never been a time like it.

For this reason alone, it's not surprising that David came to symbolize all of Israel's hopes for the future. The Golden Age was the touchstone of their national imagination, the one point in the past when everything was right with their world.[1]

---

[1] Except, of course, that it wasn't. As we've already mentioned, David fell into serious sin in his later years, committing adultery and murder, and as a result his kingdom became plagued with family strife and attempted coups by several of his sons. Solomon opened the floodgates to idolatry in Jerusalem. Upon Solomon's death, the kingdom split into north and south, and the Golden Age was over. Although the temple was in Jerusalem, the people did not remain faithful to the worship of Yahweh who dwelt there. The Golden Age

But there is another reason that Messianic hopes came to hang on David's lineage, and it was much more scripturally rooted than any romanticized vision of the past. That reason was the Davidic covenant itself—the promises God had made directly to David, the progenitor of the royal line.

The Davidic covenant is found in the books of 2 Samuel 7 and 1 Chronicles 17. David had just expressed his desire to build a permanent temple for the Lord in Jerusalem that would replace the traveling tabernacle, which had served as the locus of God's presence in Israel since the time of Moses but which had a bad habit of getting misplaced. In return, God commanded the prophet Nathan to tell David:

> The Lord declares to you: The Lord Himself will make a house for you. When your time comes and you rest with your fathers, I will raise up after you your descendant, who will come from your body, and I will establish his kingdom. He will build a house for My name, and I will establish the throne of his kingdom forever. I will be a father to him, and he will be a son to Me. When he does wrong, I will discipline him with a human rod and with blows from others. But My faithful love will never leave him as I removed it from Saul; I removed him from your way. Your house and kingdom will endure before Me for-

---

did not see the kingdom of God in its perfection. Nevertheless, it became a symbol of the kingdom of God and of everything that Israel could and should be. It functioned in the Israelite imagination in the same way that Eden does, or that some people today might think of romanticized, gilded visions of certain eras in the past—Arthurian Britain or Renaissance Italy, for example.

ever, and your throne will be established forever.[2]

The parallel language in 1 Chronicles 17 clearly links the kingdom of God and the kingdom of David. Speaking of David's kingly descendant, it renders the last verse:

I will appoint him *over My house and My kingdom* forever, and his throne will be established forever.[3]

In later passages, these promises are clearly applied first to Solomon and then to the line of kings who descended from him. In the exile to Babylon, David's family lost the throne. Yet, the promises of God still stood, and the prophets understood that a future Davidic king would come who would be the total fulfillment of this covenant. They prophesied exactly that. And just as 1 Chronicles 17 indicates, the coming of the Son of David was expected to dovetail with the return of the Lord and the beginning of *his* reign—the rule of the kingdom of God.

Isaiah, of course, had plenty to say about this future king who would sit on David's throne.

> For a child will be born for us,
> a son will be given to us,
> and the government will be on His shoulders.
> He will be named
> Wonderful Counselor, Mighty God,[4]

---

[2] 2 Samuel 7:11b–16
[3] 1 Chronicles 17:14, my emphasis.
[4] This name was not understood by the Jewish people to mean the coming king would *be* God. Instead, it was seen to imply that God's power and might would be displayed in and through him. Other Jewish names had similar functions: *Daniel*, "Judge of God" or "God is my Judge"; *Ezekiel*, "God strengthens"; *Elijah*, "Yah is God"; or *Joshua*, which is the Hebrew form of *Jesus*, meaning "Yahweh saves."

> Eternal Father, Prince of Peace.
> The dominion will be vast,
> and its prosperity will never end.
> He will reign on the throne of David
> and over his kingdom,
> to establish and sustain it
> with justice and righteousness from now on and forever.
> The zeal of the Lord of Hosts will accomplish this.[5]

Another prophecy from Isaiah emphasizes the Messianic Age and the Davidic king's just and peaceful influence over the nations. It also stressed that, like David, this king would delight in the law of God, and in his days knowledge of God would spread throughout the land:

> Then a shoot will grow from the stump of Jesse,
> and a branch from his roots will bear fruit.
> The Spirit of the Lord will rest on Him—
> a Spirit of wisdom and understanding,
> a Spirit of counsel and strength,
> a Spirit of knowledge and of the fear of the Lord.
> His delight will be in the fear of the Lord.
> He will not judge
> by what He sees with His eyes,
> He will not execute justice
> by what He hears with His ears,
> but He will judge the poor righteously
> and execute justice for the oppressed of the land.
> He will strike the land
> with discipline from His mouth,
> and He will kill the wicked
> with a command from His lips.

---

5 Isaiah 9:6–7

> Righteousness will be a belt around His loins;
> faithfulness will be a belt around His waist.
> The wolf will live with the lamb,
> and the leopard will lie down with the goat.
> The calf, the young lion, and the fatling will be together,
> and a child will lead them.
> The cow and the bear will graze,
> their young ones will lie down together,
> and the lion will eat straw like the ox.
> An infant will play beside the cobra's pit,
> and a toddler will put his hand into a snake's den.
> None will harm or destroy another
> on My entire holy mountain,
> for the land will be as full
> of the knowledge of the Lord
> as the sea is filled with water.
> On that day the root of Jesse
> will stand as a banner for the peoples.
> The nations will seek Him,
> and His resting place will be glorious.[6]

Nor was Isaiah the only one to speak about the coming Son of David whose reign would be enmeshed with the kingdom of God. Ezekiel did too, emphasizing that the Son of David would arise when God forgave and cleansed his people from the sins that had placed them under a curse and renewed his covenant with them to be their God and claim them as his people.

This is what the Lord God says: I am going to take the Israelites out of the nations where they have gone. I will gather them from all around and bring them into

---
[6] Isaiah 11:1–10

their own land. I will make them one nation in the land, on the mountains of Israel, *and one king will rule over all of them* ... They will not defile themselves anymore with their idols, their detestable things, and all their transgressions. I will save them from all their apostasies by which they sinned, and I will cleanse them. Then they will be My people, and I will be their God. *My servant David will be king over them, and there will be one shepherd for all of them.* They will follow My ordinances, and keep My statutes and obey them. They will live in the land that I gave to My servant Jacob, where your fathers lived. *They will live in it forever with their children and grandchildren, and My servant David will be their prince forever.* I will make a covenant of peace with them; it will be an everlasting covenant with them. I will establish and multiply them and will set My sanctuary among them forever. My dwelling place will be with them; I will be their God, and they will be My people. When My sanctuary is among them forever, the nations will know that I, Yahweh, sanctify Israel.[7]

Several other prophets also wrote about the Son of David, including Zechariah, who drew a vivid picture of the future king's arrival in Jerusalem:

Rejoice greatly, Daughter Zion! Shout in triumph, Daughter Jerusalem! Look, your King is coming to you; He is righteous and victorious, humble and riding on a donkey, on a colt, the foal of a donkey ... His dominion will extend from sea to sea, from the Euphrates River to the ends of the earth.[8]

---

7 Ezekiel 37:21–22a, 23–28, my emphasis.
8 Zechariah 9:9, 10b

But perhaps the most powerful of the Son of David prophecies were found in the psalms, in two small songs probably written by David himself.

The first of these, Psalm 2, emphasizes several important ideas. First, it actually uses the Hebrew term "Messiah" in verse 2, where the English reads "Anointed One." This is the first place in Scripture where the ideas of kingship and Messiahship are tied together. Second, it hearkened back to the covenantal promise found in 2 Samuel 7:14 that "I will be a father to him, and he will be a son to Me." Third—and importantly to the oppressed Jewish people in John the Baptist's day, who were weary from centuries of oppression by foreign powers—it stressed the idea of military victory and dominance over the nations, including the enemies of Israel and of God.

> Here is the psalm in its entirety:
> Why do the nations rebel
> and the peoples plot in vain?
> The kings of the earth take their stand,
> and the rulers conspire together
> against the Lord and His Anointed One:
> "Let us tear off their chains
> and free ourselves from their restraints."
> The One enthroned in heaven laughs;
> the Lord ridicules them.
> Then He speaks to them in His anger
> and terrifies them in His wrath:
> "I have consecrated My King
> on Zion, My holy mountain."
> I will declare the Lord's decree:
> He said to Me, "You are My Son;
> today I have become Your Father.

> Ask of Me,
> and I will make the nations Your inheritance
> and the ends of the earth Your possession.
> You will break them with a rod of iron;
> You will shatter them like pottery."
> So now, kings, be wise;
> receive instruction, you judges of the earth.
> Serve the Lord with reverential awe
> and rejoice with trembling.
> Pay homage to the Son or He will be angry
> and you will perish in your rebellion,
> for His anger may ignite at any moment.
> All those who take refuge in Him are happy.

Other prophets and writers also stressed this element of God's warlike victory. Zephaniah, for example, wrote "Do not fear; Zion, do not let your hands grow weak. Yahweh your God is among you, a warrior who saves."[9] Micah is more violent, connecting Yahweh's victory to the victory of Israel over their enemies: "Rise and thresh, Daughter Zion, for I will make your horns iron and your hooves bronze, so you can crush many peoples. Then you will set apart their plunder to the Lord for destruction, their wealth to the Lord of all the earth."[10]

Isaiah too pictures God arising violently to take vengeance on the nations who unjustly oppress his people:

> Justice is turned back,
> and righteousness stands far off.
> For truth has stumbled in the public square,
> and honesty cannot enter.
> Truth is missing,

---

9 Zephaniah 3:16b–17
10 Micah 4:13

and whoever turns from evil is plundered.
The Lord saw that there was no justice,
and He was offended.
He saw that there was no man—
He was amazed that there was no one interceding;
so His own arm brought salvation,
and His own righteousness supported Him.
He put on righteousness like a breastplate,
and a helmet of salvation on His head;
He put on garments of vengeance for clothing,
and He wrapped Himself in zeal as in a cloak.
So He will repay according to their deeds:
fury to His enemies,
retribution to His foes,
and He will repay the coastlands.
They will fear the name of Yahweh in the west
and His glory in the east;
for He will come like a rushing stream
driven by the wind of the Lord.
"The Redeemer will come to Zion,
and to those in Jacob who turn from transgression."
This is the Lord's declaration.[11]

The second of the major Messianic psalms, Psalm 110, links this expectation of victory and vanquishing of enemies even more strongly with the coming Davidic king than Psalm 2 does. It also introduces the idea of this king as a priest—not from the family of Levi (as all Israelite priests were) but belonging to another, older and more mysterious "lineage." As the builders of the temple and lovers of the law, David and Solomon had both behaved in priest-like ways at times, introducing

---

[11] Isaiah 59:14–20

the idea within Israel's history that priesthood and kingship might go hand in hand.[12] In the future, according to Psalm 110, this possibility would come to pass. Notice the interplay of "Lord" (Hebrew *Yahweh,* the God of Israel) and "Lord" (Hebrew *Adonai,* meaning a ruler—divine or earthly) in this psalm:

> This is the declaration of the Lord
> to my Lord:
> "Sit at My right hand
> until I make Your enemies Your footstool."
> The Lord will extend Your mighty scepter from Zion.
> Rule over Your surrounding enemies.
> Your people will volunteer
> on Your day of battle.
> In holy splendor, from the womb of the dawn,
> the dew of Your youth belongs to You.
> The Lord has sworn an oath and will not take it back:
> "Forever, You are a priest
> like Melchizedek."
> The Lord is at Your right hand;
> He will crush kings on the day of His anger.
> He will judge the nations, heaping up corpses;
> He will crush leaders over the entire world.
> He will drink from the brook by the road;
> therefore, He will lift up His head.

All of these prophecies and psalms paint a strong picture of a future human king from David's family who would be linked to the redemption of Israel from the power of sin and the curse, the vanquishing of Israel's enemies, and the coming—on earth—of the kingdom of

---

12 G.K. Beale, *A New Testament Biblical Theology: The Unfolding of the Old Testament in the New* (Grand Rapids: Baker Academic, 2011), 71.

God. Viewing them together, we can see where Jesus's contemporaries got their expectations of the Messiah as a warrior king who would defeat Rome and set up an earthly throne in Jerusalem. And Psalm 110, with its exalted, divine language, begins to hint at a more supernatural element to this king's story as well.

But we have further to go in understanding the expectations of John the Baptist and others in his world. There is one more Old Testament vision we need to visit, and it's stranger and more fascinating than anything we've seen yet.

I'm speaking, of course, of Daniel.

Chapter 5:
What John Believed: The Apocalypse of Daniel

If Isaiah draws a picture of a peaceful, Edenic new age filled with harmony and justice under the rule of the Davidic "Branch," and the psalms paint an image of an iron-fisted ruler crushing his enemies, Daniel introduces a new element entirely to the mosaic of the Messiah.

Reading the book of Daniel, we immediately become aware that something has shifted in the biblical narrative. In reality, several things have.

First, unlike the psalms and prophecies penned in the Holy Land, Daniel was written in Babylon.[1] Its author was the prophet Daniel, a young Jewish nobleman who was carried into exile in the first wave of Babylonian conquest about a hundred years after Isaiah lived and wrote. Its central theme is not warning about a future judgment but a quest to remain personally faithful to God in the midst of that judgment, and it is graced by the discovery that *God* is present and faithful even when

---

1 Scholars debate the authorship and dating of Daniel; on both, I take a traditional position.

one is surrounded by enemies and has become a stranger in a strange land. Its language feels different even in English translations, for good reason: in several of the book's chapters, the underlying language is not Hebrew but Aramaic, reflecting a linguistic change that was underway in the Jewish communities the time.[2]

The book of Daniel is part autobiography, part prophecy. But the prophetic portions of Daniel are quite different from anything we've encountered in the Old Testament so far. This is because they belong to another genre, one seen in a less developed form only a few other places in the Old Testament, especially in Isaiah, Ezekiel, and Zechariah. That genre was called *apocalyptic,* from the Greek word *apocalypse.* Apocalyptic is a poetic, visionary genre heavy with symbolism and coded meaning. It was often written in contexts of oppression, where coding might have helped the writers escape charges of sedition by the ruling powers of the time. This probably helps explain why Daniel and Ezekiel, both of whom lived and wrote in Babylon, used it—as did John in the New Testament book of Revelation, writing while he was in exile under the rule of Rome. But it was also ideal for capturing transcendent spiritual realities that

---

[2] Aramaic is a Semitic language, closely related to Hebrew but not identical to it. It was spoken as a trade language throughout the Mesopotamian world, and during the exile in Babylon, it became the primary language of the exiled community. When the exiles returned to Israel after the exile, the Bible records that Ezra and the Levites could not simply read the law out loud to the people; they had to "translate and give the meaning so that the people could understand what was read" (Nehemiah 8:8)—most likely because they no longer clearly understood Hebrew. By the time of Jesus, Aramaic was the primary language spoken by Jewish people within the Holy Land, including by Jesus himself.

existed over and against material realities. In Greek, *apocalypse* means "unveiling" or "revelation." As a genre, apocalyptic helped readers look past the realities of the physical world to the spiritual dimension behind them.

As a faithful worshiper of Yahweh, Daniel sought God and had astounding experiences with him—made all the more powerful and poignant by the fact that he was in exile at the time. And God revealed a great deal about the future to him, especially showing him how the great drama of judgment and curse, redemption and restoration, and the coming of the kingdom of God would play out.

Over time, three chapters of Daniel became especially significant to Jewish expectations of the future, the Messiah, and the Messianic Age. All three relayed supernatural visions and prophecies in the rich, sometimes bizarre language of apocalyptic.

And all three hinted at a spiritual dimension to future events that challenged and excited those who studied them in the years to come. *There are more things in heaven and Earth, Horatio, / Than are dreamt of in your philosophy.*

PARALLEL VISIONS:
STATUES AND A STONE, MONSTERS AND A MAN

The first of these chapters is Daniel 2. It starts out as biography: Nebuchadnezzar, the incredibly powerful and psychopathic ruler of the Babylonian Empire, had a profoundly disturbing dream and called on all his advisors and magicians to use their supposed supernatural insight to interpret it. First, though, he refused to tell them what the dream *was*. He would trust their interpretation only if they first accurately relayed his own secret thoughts to him.

The advisors and magicians protested (naturally), and Nebuchadnezzar ordered them all executed. Fortunately for everyone, the category of "advisors and magicians" included Daniel and several other young Hebrew men in exile, who had been brought into the king's household and trained up as professional wise men. When the executioners arrived at Daniel's door, Daniel asked what was going on and sent word back to the king that if he would hold off on killing everyone, Daniel would be able to interpret the dream—he just needed time to seek the God of heaven first.[3]

Although the book does not specify exactly when, Daniel got his answer from God quickly. "The mystery was then revealed to Daniel in a vision at night, and Daniel praised the God of heaven."[4] Daniel then went before King Nebuchadnezzar and told him his dream—a dream, Daniel declared, that revealed the future.

> My king, as you were watching, a colossal statue appeared. That statue, tall and dazzling, was stand-

---

[3] "God of heaven" is a phrase found primarily in Daniel and the books of Ezra and Nehemiah, which were written during the period of return from exile when the people of Israel were under Persian rule. It's an interesting departure from the more common biblical term "God of Israel," and it might be seen both as a kind of cross-cultural bridging—Daniel, Ezra, and Nehemiah use the term "God of heaven" when speaking to pagan kings, and the pagan kings likewise use it to refer to Israel's God—and perhaps as a broadening of their understanding. Their God is not, after all, *only* the God of Israel. As Jewish liturgy even today has it, he is "the King of the universe."

[4] Daniel 2:19

ing in front of you, and its appearance was terrifying. The head of the statue was pure gold, its chest and arms were silver, its stomach and thighs were bronze, its legs were iron, and its feet were partly iron and partly fired clay. As you were watching, a stone broke off without a hand touching it, struck the statue on its feet of iron and fired clay, and crushed them. Then the iron, the fired clay, the bronze, the silver, and the gold were shattered and became like chaff from the summer threshing floors. The wind carried them away, and not a trace of them could be found. But the stone that struck the statue became a great mountain and filled the whole earth.[5]

Daniel went on to interpret the dream. Each distinct material in the statue, he said, represented a great kingdom, beginning with Babylon—the head of gold. After Babylon fell, three other kingdoms or empires would arise, represented by the silver and bronze and finally the legs of iron. The last would be most terrible of all, "for iron crushes and shatters everything, and like iron that smashes, it will crush and smash all the others."[6] The feet and toes of mixed iron and clay represented a fundamental instability in this final kingdom, however, apparently brought on by the multinational extent of its rule: though it would rule many peoples, they would not properly cohere. "You saw the iron mixed with clay—the peoples will mix with one another but will not hold together, just as iron does not mix with fired clay."[7]

---

5 Daniel 2:31–35
6 Daniel 2:40
7 Daniel 2:43

It was the last part of the vision, though, that mattered most. God was revealing to Nebuchadnezzar—and to Daniel, and to all who would read Daniel's words—that one day all human empires would fall, even the most powerful. And the agent of their fall would be small and simple, a stone cut out of a mountain without the work of human hands. It would destroy the greatest works of idolatrous, empire-building human beings. This stone, Daniel explained, would be the kingdom of God itself.

> In the days of those kings, the God of heaven will set up a kingdom that will never be destroyed, and this kingdom will not be left to another people. It will crush all these kingdoms and bring them to an end, but will itself endure forever. You saw a stone break off from the mountain without a hand touching it, and it crushed the iron, bronze, fired clay, silver, and gold. The great God has told the king what will happen in the future. The dream is true, and its interpretation certain.[8]

For Daniel, the story ended well—he not only escaped execution but was also honored and promoted by Nebuchadnezzar, who was probably relieved to hear the stone would not strike the statue in his own day. (Somewhat ironically, the next story in Daniel has Nebuchadnezzar building a giant golden statue and demanding that everyone in the kingdom bow down and worship it—not quite the inspiration he was supposed to take from the dream.)

But another dream was in store, this one given directly to Daniel. Parallel in its shape and reaching a simi-

---

8 Daniel 2:44–45

lar conclusion, this one was far more lurid in its details and detailed in its scope. Interestingly, when Daniel had this dream, Babylon was on the cusp of falling—it would soon be taken over in the middle of the night by the kingdom of the Medes and Persians.

Daniel's vision begins at the opening of chapter 7:

> In the first year of Belshazzar king of Babylon, Daniel had a dream with visions in his mind as he was lying in his bed. He wrote down the dream, and here is the summary of his account. Daniel said, "In my vision at night I was watching, and suddenly the four winds of heaven stirred up the great sea. Four huge beasts came up from the sea, each different from the other."

The chapter goes on to describe these terrible beasts. They were not simply animals, but monstrous, deformed creatures that live to terrorize and dominate, gorging themselves on the flesh of their victims. Just as there were four types of building material in Nebuchadnezzar's statue, there were four monsters in Daniel's vision. And once again, the worst of them was the last. Note, too, the recurrence of "iron" as a motif:

> While I was watching in the night visions, a fourth beast appeared, frightening and dreadful, and incredibly strong, with large iron teeth. It devoured and crushed, and it trampled with its feet whatever was left. It was different from all the beasts before it, and it had 10 horns.[9]

While Daniel watched, suddenly a little horn came

---
9 Daniel 7:7

up from among the original ten on the great iron beast. This horn was small, but it had eyes like a man's, "and it had a mouth that spoke arrogantly."[10]

Because of its connection with powerful animals like bulls, rams, and oxen, in biblical imagery the "horn" is always an image of power, of brute strength. Therefore, the phrase "little horn" may imply one who lacked real strength. In this case, it relied instead on threatening and perhaps blasphemous or deceptive words for power. Yet the horn was able to do great damage, employing the strength of the iron beast to devour and destroy.

Whatever the case, at this point Daniel's terrifying vision took an unexpected turn. Apparently provoked by the arrogant words of the "little horn," the scene suddenly shifted, giving way to one of the most awe-inspiring moments in Scripture: the sudden convening of a heavenly court, with God himself as the Judge.

> "As I kept watching," Daniel said,
> thrones were set in place,
> and the Ancient of Days took His seat.
> His clothing was white like snow,
> and the hair of His head like whitest wool.
> His throne was flaming fire;
> its wheels were blazing fire.
> A river of fire was flowing,
> coming out from His presence.
> Thousands upon thousands served Him;
> ten thousand times ten thousand stood before Him.
> The court was convened,
> and the books were opened.[11]

---

10 Daniel 7:8
11 Daniel 7:9–10

With God now sitting as Judge, justice was swift. The little horn was deposed and destroyed; the iron beast was killed and its body burned. But then something even more wondrous and mysterious took place, something almost unbelievably strange:

> I continued watching in the night visions,
> and I saw One like a son of man
> coming with the clouds of heaven.
> He approached the Ancient of Days
> and was escorted before Him.
> He was given authority to rule,
> and glory, and a kingdom;
> so that those of every people,
> nation, and language
> should serve Him.
> His dominion is an everlasting dominion
> that will not pass away,
> and His kingdom is one
> that will not be destroyed.[12]

When Nebuchadnezzar had his dream, he was deeply disturbed and sought an interpreter. Daniel, interestingly, did the same. "Deeply distressed" and "terrified" by the visions, he approached a mysterious angelic being standing nearby and asked for an interpretation of what he had seen. Thankfully, the angel was obliging:

> So he let me know the interpretation of these things: "These huge beasts, four in number, are four kings who will rise from the earth. But the holy ones of the Most High will receive the kingdom and possess it forever, yes, forever and ever."[13]

---

[12] Daniel 7:13–14
[13] Daniel 7:16b–18

This simple interpretive key made it clear that Daniel's vision was the same as Nebuchadnezzar's. The four beasts were four kings or kingdoms—ruling powers, reigning on earth but perhaps empowered by something more frightening and unholy. The Son of Man in the vision, who appeared among the monsters like Daniel in the lion's den and who was brought before the Judge on his throne, represented not a person but a *people*, the holy ones (or saints) of the Most High. After the monsters had had their day, the people of God would be given an everlasting kingdom, never to be lost or taken from them. Fantastically, they would even seem to rule alongside God, sharing in his power and authority.

Not satisfied with this answer, Daniel pressed for more understanding of the fourth beast, "the one different from all the others, extremely terrifying, with iron teeth and bronze claws, devouring, crushing, and trampling with its feet whatever was left."[14] He also expressed a little more about what he had seen in the rise of the little horn:

> As I was watching, this horn waged war against the holy ones and was prevailing over them until the Ancient of Days arrived and a judgment was given in favor of the holy ones of the Most High, for the time had come, and the holy ones took possession of the kingdom.[15]

Before being given the kingdom, Daniel indicated, the holy ones would suffer beneath the rule of the monsters and even be nearly defeated by the little horn. The

---

14 Daniel 7:20
15 Daniel 7:22

angel agreed with this. After giving Daniel more detail about the fourth beast and little horn, he warned:

> He will speak words against the Most High and oppress the holy ones of the Most High. He will intend to change religious festivals and laws, and the holy ones will be handed over to him for a time, times, and half a time.[16]

Nevertheless, this season would be limited. Daniel was to keep his hope in the justice of God, which would surely come:

> But the court will convene, and his dominion will be taken away, to be completely destroyed forever. The kingdom, dominion, and greatness of the kingdoms under all of heaven will be given to the people, the holy ones of the Most High. His kingdom will be an everlasting kingdom, and all rulers will serve and obey Him.[17]

And with that, the vision ended.

A VISION OF SUFFERING AND THE SEVENTY WEEKS

Daniel's vision introduced several new expectations for Israel's future—though to call them "hope" is a stretch. Through his vision of four successive empires, and especially of the last empire with its terrifying power and the little horn's warmongering against the people of God, he seemed to stretch out the expectation of restoration to a time yet far in the future. The era foreseen by Isaiah, Ezekiel, Micah, and others would come, but that day was yet far off.

---

16 Daniel 7:25
17 Daniel 7:27

Moreover, the last empire would make war against the saints and nearly defeat them. Literally, the little horn would "wear out" the saints,[18] and only the convening of the heavenly courts and God's direct intervention would save them. On the other hand, the vision of the Son of Man—in the angel's interpretation, the corporate people of God—being given authority, glory, and everlasting dominion was a truly hopeful one. Although it would come through a time of intense suffering, the Messianic Age would surely come.

But what about a *Messiah*? At first glance there certainly seems to be a Messianic king in Daniel's vision. He is one who "comes with the clouds of heaven" and stands before the Ancient of Days to receive the kingdom. But then both Daniel and the angel equate this figure with the corporate body of God's people: "the holy ones of the Most High."[19] So is there a Messiah here or isn't there?

To this day, that question is a cause for fair debate. But historically, most Israelite readers decided that there was.[20] After all, even a corporate kingdom needed a figurehead, someone to sit on the actual throne. Surely Daniel was seeing *both*—the victory of a people through the victory of a person who represented them.

First, though, the people would pass through a time of suffering. A natural question to follow might be, *How long?* And that is, in fact, the next question of Messianic

---

[18] Daniel 7:25
[19] Daniel 7:18, 22, 27
[20] See "Messianism: Jewish Messianism," *Encyclopedia of Religion* (Thomson Gale, 2005). Hosted at Encyclopedia.com. See also Joseph Jacobs and Moses Buttenwieser, "Messiah," *The Jewish Encyclopedia* (1906). Referenced at JewishEncyclopedia.com.

importance to be addressed in Daniel. The final prophecy we'll look at here addresses time frames. It is usually known as Daniel's Seventy Weeks.

ON THE CUSP OF A PROMISE FULFILLED

First, a little background: The book of Daniel began with the prophet's early years in Babylon, shortly after he and his friends were taken away in exile. The book intersperses apocalyptic visions with events from Daniel's life, forming a rough timeline through his promotion in Babylon to the rise of the Medes and Persians and finally, to the near end of Daniel's life. When he wrote chapter 9, he was an old man. He had lived a full and faithful life in the presence of his enemies, and God had faithfully shepherded him there. Even though Daniel had no hope of personally seeing the house of the Lord in Jerusalem rebuilt, he might say with the psalmist, "Surely goodness and mercy shall follow me all the days of my life, and I will dwell in the house of the Lord forever."[21] The God of Israel had proven to be the God of heaven—mighty, present, and ultimately asserting his just rule even over pagan oppressors.

Yet, the goodness of God in Babylon did not take away Daniel's longing for his people to be redeemed from the power of the curse. He deeply desired for them to be delivered from their enemies and restored to the land where God would dwell among them, just as Isaiah and others had prophesied. And there was in fact a time limit on the exile. It had been given through Jeremiah, a

---

21 Psalm 23:6

prophet who lived and prophesied at the very end of Judah's independence and who was present when Jerusalem fell and its people were carried away to Babylon. Jeremiah died in Egypt among Jewish refugees there—a painfully poignant circumstance for a prophet whose nation was born out of slavery in Egypt centuries before. But long before he died, Jeremiah relayed the temporal parameters on God's judgment of Israel. Like Isaiah, he stressed the continued faithfulness of God through the time of judgment and his promise to eventually restore his people.

> For this is what the Lord says: "When 70 years for Babylon are complete, I will attend to you and will confirm My promise concerning you to restore you to this place. For I know the plans I have for you"—this is the Lord's declaration—"plans for your welfare, not for disaster, to give you a future and a hope. You will call to Me and come and pray to Me, and I will listen to you. You will seek Me and find Me when you search for Me with all your heart. I will be found by you"—this is the Lord's declaration—"and I will restore your fortunes and gather you from all the nations and places where I banished you"—this is the Lord's declaration. "I will restore you to the place I deported you from."[22]

With that promise in hand, Daniel and other faithful Hebrews counted the years as they passed. And as seventy years approached, Daniel devoted himself to fast and pray—pressing into the promise of God. Chapter 9 opens, "I, Daniel, understood from the books according to the word of the Lord to Jeremiah the prophet that the

---

22 Jeremiah 29:10–14

number of years for the desolation of Jerusalem would be 70. So I turned my attention to the Lord God to seek Him by prayer and petitions, with fasting, sackcloth, and ashes."[23] In great detail, Daniel confessed the sins of Israel and poured out his heart to God, begging for his forgiveness and mercy in accordance with his word to Jeremiah.

> Now, Lord our God, who brought Your people out of the land of Egypt with a mighty hand and made Your name renowned as it is this day, we have sinned, we have acted wickedly. Lord, in keeping with all Your righteous acts, may Your anger and wrath turn away from Your city Jerusalem, Your holy mountain; for because of our sins and the iniquities of our fathers, Jerusalem and Your people have become an object of ridicule to all those around us.
>
> Therefore, our God, hear the prayer and the petitions of Your servant. Show Your favor to Your desolate sanctuary for the Lord's sake. Listen, my God, and hear. Open Your eyes and see our desolations and the city called by Your name. For we are not presenting our petitions before You based on our righteous acts, but based on Your abundant compassion. Lord, hear! Lord, forgive! Lord, listen and act! My God, for Your own sake, do not delay, because Your city and Your people are called by Your name.[24]

In answer to Daniel's heartfelt prayer, God sent an angel—Gabriel, whom Daniel had encountered in a pre-

---

23 Daniel 9:2–3
24 Daniel 9:15–19

vious vision. Gabriel answered Daniel's prayer with an enigmatic prophecy. In essence, he declared that the Lord's plans for Israel would not be accomplished in seventy years but in seventy "weeks"—literally "seventy sevens," usually understood to mean seventy sets of seven years. And in this time frame, far more than just restoration to the physical land of Israel would occur. In seventy weeks, Gabriel indicated, the Messiah would come[25]—and when he did, he would change the cosmic order of the world as Daniel knew it.

Even today, the prophecy of Seventy Weeks feels heavy with importance. Yet it remains enigmatic, and few interpreters then or now have agreed on exactly what it means. Here it is, as given in the Holman translation:

> So consider the message and understand the vision:
> Seventy weeks are decreed
> about your people and your holy city—
> to bring the rebellion to an end,
> to put a stop to sin,

---

[25] Today, most Bible readers understand this passage to predict the rise of the antichrist and the Second Coming of Christ. But from the time of Daniel onward, including in the early church and in Christianity generally until the late 1800s, it was understood to be speaking of the Messiah's *first* coming. The reference to destruction is then understood to refer to the devastating fall of Jerusalem under the Roman general Titus in AD 70. The prophecy only became popularly associated with the future when C.I. Scofield published his popular reference Bible in 1909 and 1917, giving his futurist interpretation of the passage in the accompany margin commentary. See Roger T. Beckwith, "Daniel 9 and the Date of Messiah's Coming in Essene, Hellenistic, Pharisaic, Zealot and Early Christian Computation," *Revue De Qumrân10,* no. 4 (40) (1981): 521-42. jstor.org/stable/24607004. See also George F. Moore, "Fourteen Generations: 490 Years: An Explanation of the Genealogy of Jesus," *The Harvard Theological Review* 14, no. 1 (1921): 97-103. jstor.org/stable/1507663.

to wipe away iniquity,
to bring in everlasting righteousness,
to seal up vision and prophecy,
and to anoint the most holy place.
Know and understand this:
From the issuing of the decree
to restore and rebuild Jerusalem
until Messiah the Prince
will be seven weeks and 62 weeks.
It will be rebuilt with a plaza and a moat,
but in difficult times.
After those 62 weeks
the Messiah will be cut off
and will have nothing.
The people of the coming prince
will destroy the city and the sanctuary.
The end will come with a flood,
and until the end there will be war;
desolations are decreed.
He will make a firm covenant
with many for one week,
but in the middle of the week
he will put a stop to sacrifice and offering.
And the abomination of desolation
will be on a wing of the temple
until the decreed destruction
is poured out on the desolator.[26]

Seventy Weeks and the Jubilee of Jubilees

One frequently overlooked characteristic of the Seventy Weeks passage is the structure of Jubilee built into

---

26 Daniel 9:15–19

it.[27] In the Mosaic covenant, God had given the people of Israel a calendar based around religious feasts and festivals, of which the most regular was the sabbath—a day "made holy," set apart, for rest. The sabbath was observed every seventh day. Not only the people but also their animals were to rest on the sabbath day, in honor of God's rest after creating the world in Genesis 2:1–3.[28]

The sabbath, however, also extended into seven-year patterns—"sevens." Every seven years, the sabbath was to extend to the holy land itself: the Jewish people were to allow the land to lie fallow for an entire year. *Rest* was an integral part of their stewardship of the land and a primary way they acknowledged God's ultimate ownership of it. Finally, an even greater event was to take place after every seven *sevens*, or "seven weeks" as it is translated in Leviticus 25 and elsewhere. This event was called the Jubilee, and it began on the Day of Atonement at the end of every forty-nine years—that is, the end of every "seven sevens."[29]

Jubilee encompassed the entire fiftieth year. It was not only a sabbath year, but it was also a year of tremendous and nationwide *restoration*. Across the land, debts were forgiven and canceled out. Land—which was originally parceled out by lot to the tribes of Israel and belonged to each of Israel's families as a birthright under

---

27 See Mitchell L. Chase, "What Are the Seventy Weeks of Daniel? (Daniel 9)," Crossway.org. Article adapted from *ESV Expository Commentary: Daniel–Malachi: Volume 7*, edited by Iain M. Duguid, James M. Hamilton Jr, and Jay Sklar. crossway.org/articles/what-are-the-seventy-weeks-of-daniel-daniel-9. See also Dean R. Ulrich, "The Need for More Attention to Jubilee in Daniel 9:24–27," *Bulletin for Biblical Research 26*, no. 4 (2016): 481-500. jstor.org/stable/26371526.
28 Exodus 20:10
29 See Leviticus 25.

God—was restored to the families who had originally owned it, after having been sold or bartered away or lost through indebtedness or incompetence. And all across the land, slaves were set free.

It's significant that in Jewish culture under the Old Covenant, slavery was often specifically tied to debt. Jewish slaves served limited terms, and they did so mostly for the sake of repaying debt or atoning for a crime (for example, someone who had stolen from someone else and was not able to repay it would become a slave to the offended party until the debt was paid back, plus some extra). The connection to crime was a tacit acknowledgment that sin against one's neighbor is a form of debt, and that debt leads naturally to captivity. But in the Jubilee, grace reigned. No matter how much time might remain to be served, on that forty-ninth Day of Atonement every Jewish slave was released from his sins, his debts, and his captivity and restored to freedom and full inheritance among the people of God.[30]

As several scholars have pointed out, Gabriel's use of the term "seventy weeks" at the beginning of the prophecy is clearly meant to give the whole passage of time a Jubilee structure.[31] And indeed, seventy sevens leads

---

30 Some slaves chose to remain with their masters, "out of love," according to Deuteronomy 15:16. There's probably an important picture for us in that too, but a different one than is seen in the Jubilee.
31 Again, see Mitchell L. Chase, "What Are the Seventy Weeks of Daniel? (Daniel 9)," Crossway.org. Article adapted from *ESV Expository Commentary: Daniel–Malachi: Volume 7*, edited by Iain M. Duguid, James M. Hamilton Jr, and Jay Sklar. crossway.org/articles/what-are-the-seventy-weeks-of-daniel-daniel-9. See also Dean R. Ulrich, "The Need for More Attention to Jubilee in Daniel 9:24–27," *Bulletin for Biblical Research 26*, no. 4 (2016): 481-500. jstor.org/stable/26371526.

to 490 years, "a Jubilee of Jubilees" in biblical numbering, where the number 7 (for perfection and rest) is multiplied and magnified by the number 10 (signifying completion, authority, and divine order).[32] And just as might be expected in a Jubilee of Jubilees, the seventy sevens would cancel all debts and bring about a tremendous work of forgiveness, freedom, and restoration. According to the angel, the period of seventy weeks would "bring the rebellion to an end, put a stop to sin, wipe away iniquity, bring in everlasting righteousness, seal up vision and prophecy, and anoint the most holy place"[33] (literally, "to anoint the most holy"; the word *place* is added in most English translations).

The book of Daniel ends with further prophecies and apocalyptic visions of the future, especially dealing with the empires of Persia and Greece. Finally, chapter 12 closes the book—and Daniel's story—with an angelic benediction. "Go your way, Daniel," an angel says:

> For the words are secret and sealed until the time of the end. Many will be purified, cleansed, and refined, but the wicked will act wickedly; none of the wicked will understand, but the wise will understand ... But as for you, go on your way to the end; you will rest, then rise to your destiny at the end of the days.[34]

As I said at the beginning of this section, the visions of Daniel added a new element to Israel's understanding of the Messiah. This element is Daniel's almost spooky

---

32 See graceintorah.net/2015/06/15/hebrew-numbers-1-10
33 Daniel 9:24
34 Daniel 12:9–10, 13

supernaturalism. Yes, Gabriel explained much of the symbolism; yes, it's possible to read all three chapters without even seeing a Messiah at all. Possible—but not easy. And in fact, it is hard to read Daniel's visions without asking the question—in some mysterious way, could the Messiah himself be divine?

Interestingly, this question *was* asked by Jewish readers and thinkers in the days before Jesus. What precisely they meant by it is not clear; they speculated as to whether "Bar Nash"—the "Son of Man"—might be a preexistent being, perhaps an incredibly powerful angel.[35] They didn't have answers, only questions. But the question was not outside the realm of possibility.

Looking to the Future—Again

As Jeremiah had predicted, after seventy years of exile in Babylon the Israelite people did begin to return home. Under the Persian king Cyrus, they were granted permission to return to their own land and even to rebuild Jerusalem and the temple in its midst. Cyrus, in fact, commissioned them to build the temple to Yahweh—an incredible turn of events, one foretold in Isaiah with emphasis on its extreme improbability.[36]

But it quickly became apparent that Daniel's longer time frame would also hold true. Although the exiles returned and rebuilt their city and temple under the leadership of Nehemiah and Ezra, other pivotal aspects

---
35 See Joseph Jacobs and Moses Buttenwieser, "Messiah," *The Jewish Encyclopedia* (1906). Referenced at JewishEncyclopedia.com.
36 See Isaiah 44:24–45:1–25; Ezra 1:1–2

of the restoration prophecies were not fulfilled. The enemies of the nation were not destroyed. Its pagan overlords continued to rule. Zerubbabel, a leader among the returned community who was a direct descendant of David, did not become king. While he was chosen by God, it was clear he was not the Messiah. The renewed Golden Age seemed as far away as ever.[37]

Most importantly, the rebuilt temple *lacked the glorious presence of God*.[38] Isaiah and Ezekiel, among others, had clearly declared that Yahweh would return to his people and dwell among them, with such a powerful presence that the knowledge of God would "fill the earth as the waters cover the sea."[39] Ezekiel, who witnessed the presence of God leaving the first temple in a vision (described in Ezekiel 10), also wrote of a day when God's presence would fill and even overflow a glorious new temple in Jerusalem:

> He led me to the gate, the one that faces east, and I saw the glory of the God of Israel coming from the

---

37 I first saw this pointed out by N.T. Wright in *The New Testament and the People of God* (Minneapolis: Fortress Press, 1992).
38 Ibid. The glory was not the only thing missing. Multiple markers of God's presence failed to be manifest in the new temple. Referencing rabbinic sources, commentator John Gill listed those things which were considered to be lacking in the new temple: "The Jews themselves own there were several things wanting in the latter which were in the former, as the 'ark', the 'Urim' and 'Thummim', the 'fire' from heaven, the 'Shechinah' (or, as in some books, the anointing oil, and, in others, the cherubim), and the 'Holy Ghost': by one of their writers, they are reckoned in this order, the ark, the mercy seat, and cherubim, one; the Shechinah or divine Majesty, the second; the Holy Ghost, which is prophecy, the third; Urim and Thummim the fourth: and the fire from heaven the fifth." (John Gill, "Haggai 2:9," *John Gill's Exposition of the Bible*. Hosted at BibleStudyTools.com.)
39 Habakkuk 2:14, KJV

east. His voice sounded like the roar of mighty waters, and the earth shone with His glory. I fell facedown. The glory of the Lord entered the temple by way of the gate that faced east. Then the Spirit lifted me up and brought me to the inner court, and the glory of the Lord filled the temple.[40]

Certainly, when the Jewish community under Nehemiah and Ezra returned to the land, they hoped this prophecy would be fulfilled in the temple they rebuilt. But just as their Davidic contemporary Zerubbabel became a respected leader but never ascended the throne, so the temple became the respected center of Jewish worship of Yahweh again, and yet lacked the presence of God in the way it had formerly dwelt there.

As the returned exiles regarded the temple in the process of being rebuilt and felt the sting of its strange emptiness, Haggai declared the word of the Lord:

"Speak to Zerubbabel son of Shealtiel, governor of Judah, to the high priest Joshua son of Jehozadak, and to the remnant of the people: *Who is left among you who saw this house in its former glory? How does it look to you now? Doesn't it seem like nothing to you?* Even so, be strong, Zerubbabel"—this is the Lord's declaration. "Be strong, Joshua son of Jehozadak, high priest. Be strong, all you people of the land"—this is the Lord's declaration. "Work! For I am with you"—the declaration of the Lord of Hosts. "This is the promise I made to you when you came out of Egypt, and My Spirit is present among you; don't be afraid."

---

40 Ezekiel 43:1–2, 4–5

> For the Lord of Hosts says this: "Once more, in a little while, I am going to shake the heavens and the earth, the sea and the dry land. I will shake all the nations so that the treasures of all the nations will come, *and I will fill this house with glory,"* says the Lord of Hosts. "The silver and gold belong to Me"—this is the declaration of the Lord of Hosts. *"The final glory of this house will be greater than the first,"* says the Lord of Hosts. "I will provide peace in this place"—this is the declaration of the Lord of Hosts.[41]

And so, a Daniel 9-like strain can be heard echoing in the writings of the post-exilic prophets Haggai, Zechariah, and Malachi. As N.T. Wright has pointed out, they recognized that although the seventy years had been fulfilled and the people had come home, the exile was not yet over. It would not finally end, in fact, until the Lord himself came home.

The period Daniel marked out—490 years to the Jubilee of Jubilees—became the temporal framework for Messianic expectation. For us, looking back from millennia later, it's therefore highly tempting to count. However, it's difficult, and probably unnecessary, to run exact calculations on Daniel's prophetic dates. There are several reasons for this. A big one is that all ancient dating systems are approximate. No one in the Hebrew, Greek, or Roman worlds had the kind of record-keeping systems we have now, and records were subject to decay and destruction (on the one hand) and scribal errors (on the other—and these could be just as damaging as decay!).

---

41 Haggai 2:2–9, my emphasis.

But this lack of countable dates is also not as important as it may seem at first glance. The numbers given by Daniel and even Jeremiah were rounded, apocalyptic numbers—approximate in their designation of times, exact in their prophetic meaning. Jeremiah's "seventy years" in fact only lasted sixty-seven.[42] So it's not necessary to demand that the much longer 490 years—the seventy weeks, signifying a prophetic Jubilee of Jubilees—be traceable down to the day. Suffice it to say that when Matthew laid out his genealogy of Jesus, he deliberately structured it in such a way as to claim that 490 years had passed from the exile to the birth of Jesus.[43]

Malachi encapsulated the promise of this future day, but with his promise came a warning. Just as Israel did not listen to the Lord when he warned them against destruction so, when he came, they might not be ready. A way would need to be prepared before him—a way not over rough and uneven ground but through rough and impure hearts:

> "See, I am going to send My messenger, and he will clear the way before Me. Then the Lord you seek will suddenly come to His temple, the Messenger of the covenant you desire—see, He is coming," says the Lord of Hosts. But who can endure the day of His coming? And who will be able to stand when

---

[42] See Mitchell L. Chase, "What Are the Seventy Weeks of Daniel? (Daniel 9)," Crossway.org. Article adapted from *ESV Expository Commentary: Daniel–Malachi: Volume 7*, edited by Iain M. Duguid, James M. Hamilton Jr, and Jay Sklar. crossway.org/articles/what-are-the-seventy-weeks-of-daniel-daniel-9.

[43] See George F. Moore, "Fourteen Generations: 490 Years: An Explanation of the Genealogy of Jesus," *The Harvard Theological Review* 14, no. 1 (1921): 97-103. jstor.org/stable/1507663.

He appears? For He will be like a refiner's fire and like cleansing lye. He will be like a refiner and purifier of silver; He will purify the sons of Levi and refine them like gold and silver. Then they will present offerings to the Lord in righteousness. And the offerings of Judah and Jerusalem will please the Lord as in days of old and years gone by.[44]

What John Believed

When John the Baptist arrived on the scene early in the gospels, declaring the arrival of the kingdom of God and calling on people to repent and be baptized for the forgiveness of their sins, he was clearly driven by deep convictions about what God was doing. There was a scripturally rich *content* to his faith. And although we cannot know all the nuances of what he thought or understood to be true, we can and do know what the Scriptures before him had said. Whatever precisely John expected from the Messiah, his faith found its contours in the Scriptures we've just read for ourselves. All of *this* is what John believed. The expectations set by the prophets were therefore the ground in which his doubts took root and his struggle took place.

In a couple of s, we'll look more closely at the realities of Jesus's ministry and how they clashed with John's expectations. We'll explore just why such a rock-solid man of faith might have wavered in his trust—not in God per se, but in the Galilean healer who claimed God had sent him.

---

[44] Malachi 3:1–4

But doubt is never purely an intellectual exercise. It grows up in a context not just of what we *think* but of who we *are* and what we are experiencing in our lives. So before we explore those issues more deeply, the next question to ask in our quest to understand the story of John's doubts is this one:

Who was John?

Chapter 6:
The Messenger

In our Bibles, the Old and New Testaments are separated only by a blank and a title page. We can go directly from the last words of Malachi to the first words of Matthew with hardly a pause—and so it's easy to forget what, in history, lay between those words.

According to the biblical timeline, Israel walked with God for a thousand years. During that time, the presence of God dwelt with his people in various visible and tangible ways. The prophets faithfully spoke. The Old Testament Scriptures were written. And miraculous events were part of lived Israelite experience at least every few generations. Then came the exile, and after a period of approximately seventy years the people returned from Babylon with a promise of full restoration to come after a longer span of 490 prophetic years.

And then God more or less went silent.

In Ezekiel 10, the prophet Ezekiel described God's

manifest glory departing from the temple. As we saw in our earlier look at Haggai and Malachi (who prophesied after the return from exile), even though the exiles rebuilt the temple it was clear that Yahweh had not returned—and the long silence after the handful of post-exilic prophets died only accentuated this absence.

> The silence itself had been foretold:
> Hear this! The days are coming—
> this is the declaration of the Lord God—
> when I will send a famine through the land:
> not a famine of bread or a thirst for water,
> but of hearing the words of the Lord.
> People will stagger from sea to sea
> and roam from north to east,
> seeking the word of the Lord,
> but they will not find it.[1]

Though God continued to watch over his people in notable ways, the period of silence—marked by the absence of any real prophetic voice—lasted another four hundred years or so.[2] And then, as Luke tells the story, a priest called Zechariah went to serve his yearly turn in the holy place of the temple and there encountered the angel Gabriel, the same angel who had spoken to Daniel more than five centuries before. The angel told him that he would have a son in his old age and name him John.

Moreover:

There will be joy and delight for you,

---

[1] Amos 8:11-12
[2] The prophetic significance of this should be obvious, now that we've read Daniel 9 together.

> And many will rejoice at his birth.
> For he will be great in the sight of the Lord
> And will never drink wine or beer.
> He will be filled with the Holy Spirit
> while still in his mother's womb.
> He will turn many of the sons of Israel
> To the Lord their God.
> And he will go before Him
> In the spirit and power of Elijah,
> To turn the hearts of the fathers to their children,
> And the disobedient to the understanding of the righteous,
> To make ready for the Lord a prepared people.[3]

Thirty years later, "the word of God came to John the son of Zechariah in the wilderness."[4] The famine had ended; a new era had begun.

A Life Begins ...

Despite his prominent place in the gospel story, we know very little about John's early life. He was born to elderly Levite parents somewhere in the hill country of Judea. Along with the angelic visitation that announced it, John's birth was accompanied by several miraculous events. Of course, his conception was a miracle in the first place—Elizabeth was well past menopause when he was conceived. In fact, when the angel told Zechariah he would have a son, his initial response was to express disbelief for exactly that reason. As a rebuke for his lack of faith (and also as a sign of God's involvement in the

---
3 Luke 1:14–17
4 Luke 3:2, ESV

pregnancy), the angel struck Zechariah mute, promising him that his voice would be restored after the child was born. This came to pass, but not immediately—Zechariah's voice returned only after he insisted, in writing, that the newborn boy be named John in accordance with the angel's instructions and not given a family name.[5]

According to Luke 1:15, John was filled with the Holy Spirit while still in his mother Elizabeth's womb. Finally, an event occurred before he was born that would poignantly foreshadow the days to come. Elizabeth had a young cousin named Mary, who had recently had an angelic visitation of her own—and immediately after it, she went to visit her older cousin and stay with her for the first several months of her pregnancy. The moment Mary arrived, the as-yet-unborn John responded to her presence and the presence of the child she had conceived.

When Elizabeth heard Mary's greeting, the baby leaped inside her, and Elizabeth was filled with the Holy Spirit. Then she exclaimed with a loud cry:

> "You are the most blessed of women,
> and your child will be blessed!
>
> "How could this happen to me, that the mother of my Lord should come to me? For you see, when the sound of your greeting reached my ears, the baby leaped for joy inside me! She who has believed is blessed because what was spoken to her by the Lord will be fulfilled!"[6]

---
5 See Luke 1:57–66. *John* means "Yah [or Yahweh] has been gracious."
6 Luke 1:41–45

The Desert Prophet

Although John and Jesus were relatives, the Bible does not tell us whether they spent time together in their youth. And in fact, that doesn't seem to have been the case. Mary and her husband Joseph took Jesus to Egypt when he was a young child, and after that they settled in their hometown, Nazareth in Galilee—some distance from the Judean hill country. And after his early migrations, Jesus appears to have had a fairly standard upbringing. John, on the other hand, appears to have had a highly unusual one. Most of us know John the Baptist as the fully grown man who appeared from the wilderness blazing with warnings and kingdom announcements and baptizing people in the Jordan River as a sign of repentance, cleansing, and renewal. But long before that day, he underwent a profound spiritual formation of his own in the wilderness of Judea.

Luke, who tells John's story with the most detail, does not specify at what age John left normal society and went into the Judean Desert, but he seems to have been young. Luke simply says, "The child grew up and became spiritually strong, and he was in the wilderness until the day of his public appearance to Israel."[7] Some have speculated that John lived for a while in an ascetic religious community—perhaps Qumran or somewhere like it.[8] Or he may simply have lived alone.

---

7 Luke 1:80
8 James H. Charlesworth, "John the Baptizer and Qumran," bibleodyssey.org:443/passages/related-articles/john-the-baptizer-and-qumran. Dr. Charlesworth is the former George L. Collord Professor of New Testament Language and Literature at Princeton Theological Seminary and director of the Dead Sea Scrolls Project. Although I've

Either way, John could hardly have picked a more forbidding place in which to find his spiritual footing. Lying between Jerusalem and the Dead Sea and bordered on the south by the Negev, the Judean Desert is solitary and otherworldly to this day—a dramatic landscape of deep canyons and ravines, hills and escarpments, sheer cliffs, caves, and lonely mountaintops. Hot during the day, cold and windy at night, with few edible plants and even fewer reliable water sources, it is not a hospitable place for human habitation.

Yet, even in John's day the wilderness had an ancient reputation as a place where prophets and seekers might encounter God. Many of Israel's most significant encounters had taken place not in the cities but in the desert places of the Judean wilderness and the Negev. Abraham, Isaac, and Jacob all encountered God in the wilderness while they wandered as nomads. It was in the wilderness that Moses first met Yahweh in the burning bush; and later, he was in the wilderness again when he went up on a mountain, saw the visible glory of God, and received the law. In the wilderness, God tabernacled with his people and appeared to them in cloud and fire; it was in the wilderness that he covenanted with them and constituted them as a people. David pastured his sheep as a young shepherd in the wilderness, meditated on God's law there, and received an inner revelation of God's glory, presence, and grace that remains unparal-

---

chosen not to deeply explore the possibility in this book—mostly because any conclusion I could reach would be speculative and outside of the statements of Scripture—there are several intriguing reasons to believe John was connected to the Essenes, who may have had a community at Qumran.

leled even today—and as a young man fleeing from Saul, he took refuge in the caves of the same Judean Desert where John matured from boy to prophet.

Perhaps most importantly, Elijah fled to the wilderness when his life was threatened by Jezebel and her husband Ahab, and it was in the wilderness that he heard God speak in a "still, small voice"[9]—one of the most profound and mysterious moments in all of Old Testament history.

THE JOURNEY TO CONVICTION

Whenever it was that John entered the wilderness, he embraced its harsh conditions and was shaped by them. In many ways, John's entire life was a fast, both by his choice and by God's command given through Gabriel. The angel's declaration that John would never drink beer or wine indicated that he was to be specially consecrated as a lifelong Nazirite before his birth,[10] meaning that he would be bound by a specific set of vows that were a part of Israelite religious culture. Nazirite vows, which are found in Numbers 6, could be entered into by anyone, man or woman, and were usually temporary. They were characterized by various forms of abstinence for the sake of setting oneself apart to seek God. A Nazirite vowed not to drink alcohol or eat or drink anything that derived from grapevines; cut his or her hair; or touch anything dead or unclean until the time of consecration had ended. God himself consecrated several of his

---

9 1 Kings 19:12, NKJV
10 Luke 1:15

prophets as Nazirites for life prior to their birth,[11] most notably Samuel and Samson. Consecrations of this kind were rare but always significant. They meant that God had chosen this child to be his servant as God acted in Israel. Nazirite consecration also seemed to be connected, in some way, to John's pre-birth baptism with the Holy Spirit.

To be set apart as a lifelong Nazirite meant that John was excluded from full participation in many communal gatherings. He couldn't celebrate a wedding with the customary drinking of wine or mourn a dead relative at a funeral. His long, uncut hair would have marked him visually as a man set apart from the ordinary concerns of hygiene and social acceptance. He was a living, breathing reminder that this life is not all there is, and that the call to worship God demanded one's whole life.

But John was also set apart in another way. He was a Levite, specifically descended from the priestly line. His father Zechariah served in the temple, and generations before him had done the same. This too would have shaped John's sense of identity profoundly.

Long ago, God had called the Levites to be his priests and temple servants, acting as liaisons between God and

---

[11] Interestingly, all of these consecrations were communicated through angels. Elsewhere, in the New Testament, Paul and possibly Jesus took temporary Nazirite vows; and in a particularly obscure but fascinating Old Testament case, Jephthah's daughter was likely consecrated as a lifelong Nazirite or something similar. For more on this special case, see Prof. Rabbi Jonathan Magonet, "Did Jephthah Actually Kill His Daughter?," TheTorah.com, thetorah.com/article/did-jephthah-actually-kill-his-daughter; and Miles Van Pelt, "Rethinking Jephthah's Foolish Vow," The Gospel Coalition, thegospelcoalition.org/article/rethinking-jephthah-foolish-vow.

the people of Israel. They were the set-apart tribe within a set-apart people. As part of this special vocation, the tribe of Levi paid a high price and received a higher reward: They were the only tribe out of Israel's twelve tribes not to be given a land inheritance by God. Instead, they were to live among the other tribes, teaching the people and serving God. They fulfilled temple service in Jerusalem on a rotation. And instead of land, they were to inherit God himself.[12]

Since the Levites did not have a tribal allotment of their own where they could plant and build, they lacked the resources the other tribes had. So, along with a handful of cities and fields given to them among the other tribes, they were also supported by the tithes of the nation. In this way, their living was tied to the temple and the tithe; and as such, they were a barometer for the spiritual health of Israel. Whenever the people ceased to honor God with their tithes and sacrifices, the Levites lost their ability to continue serving and had to retreat to full-time agricultural and merchant work in order to survive.

As far as we can tell, John did not serve in the temple or fulfill the usual Levitical tasks. Instead, he was set apart in the wilderness, where he was to hear from God and lead the people to repentance in preparation for Yahweh's return. On an individual scale, he fulfilled the calling of his entire tribe—to trade in earthly benefits for a heavenly inheritance and call the nation of Israel back to a holy life before God.

---

[12] Deuteronomy 18:2: "Although Levi has no inheritance among his brothers, the LORD is his inheritance, as He promised him."

As John sought God in the desert, he must have had these callings-from-birth in mind. Through no choice of his own, he had been born into the Levitical priesthood *and* consecrated in Nazirite vows. Both these ideas, of vocation and consecration, must have played into his personal sense of purpose. Certainly, he embraced them. As an ascetic, he went far beyond the usual constraints of a Nazirite. His rough clothing of camel's hair, diet of locusts and wild honey, and presumed celibacy were not a normal part of Nazirite consecration! He seems to have leaned into the idea that he was different from others and that God intended him to live his life "outside the camp" in a sense. And as he spent his days in the wilderness, that conviction began to grow and take a definite shape.

"The Prophecies Made About You"

Several decades in the future, the apostle Paul wrote to his protégé Timothy:

> Timothy, my son, I am giving you this instruction in keeping with the prophecies previously made about you, so that by them you may strongly engage in battle, having faith and a good conscience.[13]

Like Timothy, John had been given prophecies to illuminate his path in life. One prophecy had been given by the angel Gabriel when John's birth was announced; the other was spoken by his father at the moment Zechariah's voice returned.

---

13 1 Timothy 1:18–19a

"He will turn many of the sons of Israel to the Lord
their God," Gabriel had said.
> And he will go before Him
> in the spirit and power of Elijah,
> to turn the hearts of fathers
> to their children,
> and the disobedient
> to the understanding of the righteous,
> to make ready for the Lord a prepared people.[14]

Speaking by the Holy Spirit, Zechariah had addressed his prophecy directly to his newborn son:

> And child, you will be called
> a prophet of the Most High,
> for you will go before the Lord
> to prepare His ways,
> to give His people knowledge of salvation
> through the forgiveness of their sins.
> Because of our God's merciful compassion,
> the Dawn from on high will visit us
> to shine on those who live in darkness
> and the shadow of death,
> to guide our feet into the way of peace.[15]

I have to imagine John in the wilderness mulling over these words about himself. I have to imagine him weighing their meaning—speculating about the future and considering both what was in store for him and what would be required of him.

In my own life I have experienced the slow growth of a strong sense of purpose and calling, and in consid-

---
14 Luke 1:16–17
15 Luke 1:76–79

ering it I vary between disbelief and pride, wonder and panic. Perhaps you can relate. Everyone experiences the hand of the Potter in life, but once in a while we get a glimpse of the specs for the finished product—it's both a lifegiving and a terrifying thing. Living out in the desert, it seems John had plenty of time and space to consider these questions, to bathe them in prayer, and to draw near to the God who had called him. *And he needed it.* The calling on his life was not a small one. I believe deeply in God's power and desire to use "ordinary" people in "ordinary" roles to do the work of the kingdom—in fact, I think that's how God generally prefers to work. But John's calling was not ordinary in any sense of the word.

When he finally did reappear in public, John confidently proclaimed himself to be standing at the cusp of kingdom come. Without blushing, he was willing to declare himself the fulfillment of several keystone prophecies for the nation and the world. Even for a man whose birth was heralded by an angel and accompanied by powerful prophecies, convictions such as those that John held about himself and his role in history could not have formed overnight. He arrived at them through his years in the wilderness, separated from the comforts and pleasures of ordinary people. He came to them through prayer, through meditation and study of the Scriptures, and through direct divine revelation, from God's spirit to his spirit. He was not only full of the Holy Spirit, he *believed* he was full of the Holy Spirit—a condition that was not common to God's people at the time, not shared, and not without exceptionally high demands on John and his daily experience of life.

In other words, John arrived at conviction and identity in the most exacting way anyone can: he walked away from every shred of human security, threw his entire life on God, and kept pressing deeper in every practical, lived-out detail of his day-to-day existence.

THE FORERUNNER'S FORERUNNER

About four hundred years before John was born, the prophet Malachi recorded a promise from God:

> Look, I am going to send you Elijah the prophet before the great and awesome Day of the Lord comes. And he will turn the hearts of fathers to their children and children to their fathers. Otherwise, I will come and strike the land with a curse.[16]

This, of course, is what Gabriel was referencing when he said that John would "come in the spirit and power of Elijah" to prepare God's people for the return of Yahweh.

In the prophetic history of Israel, only Moses stood out as more symbolically significant than Elijah. Elijah did not write or deliver long prophetic messages like Isaiah or Jeremiah did; instead, he spoke directly to kings and rulers, usually rebuking them and declaring God's judgment on their sins. He majored in signs and wonders, even raising the dead. He shared some of John's ascetic character, being apparently unmarried and celibate and spending lengthy amounts of time in the wilderness; he was described, like John, as wearing

---
16 Malachi 4:5–6

a hairy garment with a leather belt around his waist.[17] While Isaiah seems to have been comfortable in the royal courts, and prophets like Haggai and Malachi rubbed shoulders with governors and priests, Elijah lived like an exile from polite society. His interactions with kings and princes were all elbows and sandpaper edges. He would have struck people in much the same way John the Baptist later did.

In Elijah's day, the Northern Kingdom of Israel had become deeply corrupt and paganized, largely due to the influence of King Ahab and his Sidonian wife Jezebel. The people as a whole had apostacized in such large numbers that Elijah complained to the Lord in despair that he was the only faithful Israelite left in the nation.[18] And although God was quick to correct him, his perception that he was alone does indicate how badly his people had fallen from faithfulness.

Elijah was best known for provoking a showdown with Jezebel's priests of Baal, in which he called fire down from heaven while the people shouted, "The Lord is God!"[19] And his ministry marked a significant shift in the history of Israel. In Elijah's time, judgment came on the house of Ahab. The king was killed in battle, Jezebel was thrown to her death by her own servants from an upper-story window, and a new king from a new dynasty came to power. Elijah lived during the changing of the guard and was actively involved in it. He saw out the old

---

17 2 Kings 1:8
18 1 Kings 19:14–18
19 The name *Elijah* literally means "Yah is God"; it is a shortened version of the phrase the Hebrew people shouted.

and ushered in the new by pronouncing judgment on Ahab and Jezebel and personally declaring God's choice of a new king.

But most significantly of all, Elijah encountered God as few human beings have done before or since. As I've already mentioned, on a mountain in the Negev[20] after his cataclysmic showdown with the prophets of Baal, he heard God as a "still, small voice"—one of the most profound self-disclosures in the history of God and humanity. Elijah had firsthand, direct experience of the supernatural presence of God. His entire life spoke of Holy Spirit fire, consecration, and judgment; his words and his life alike called his people to repentance and return. When the time came for his death, the writer of Kings[21] tells us that Elijah did not die. Instead, he went out into the wilderness where he had encountered God so many times before and was caught up to heaven in a chariot of fire.

The memory of all these past events and personalities were evoked by the angel's words to Zechariah that his soon-to-be-conceived son would come "in the spirit and power of Elijah" to "make ready a people prepared for the Lord." And it was true: in a spiritual sense, *John looked just like Elijah.* The two men shared a mission to call God's people away from idols and back to the worship of Yahweh, and it seems they shared a personality as well. Most of all, they shared the experience of a deeply personal revelation of God.

---

20 Scripture identifies it "the mountain of God" and "Mount Horeb." This was likely the same place as Mount Sinai, where Moses saw God and received the law.

21 Traditionally believed to be the prophet Jeremiah.

Because of Malachi, the people in his day were expecting Elijah to return in some way. John expected that too—and he believed that on some level, *he was him.*[22]

THE MESSENGER OF MALACHI AND ISAIAH

As important as it was, Malachi's Elijah prophecy was not the only prophetic role John believed he had personally been born to fulfill. Maybe even more than his connection with Elijah, John understood himself to be the messenger of Malachi and Isaiah. In the same book that includes the "return of Elijah" prophecy, Malachi wrote:

> "See, I am going to send My messenger, and he will clear the way before Me. Then the Lord you seek will suddenly come to His temple, the Messenger of the covenant you desire—see, He is coming," says the Lord of Hosts.[23]

As is usual in prophetic passages, the identity of Malachi's messenger is not clear—nor is it entirely certain if this prophecy has one messenger in mind or two. (For that matter, it's not entirely clear whether this is a "return of Yahweh" prophecy or a "coming Messiah" prophecy—or both.) Nor does Malachi explicitly connect the messenger of this prophecy with his later prophecy

---

[22] In John 1:21a, the Pharisees asked John if he was Elijah, and he explicitly answered that he was not. Yet, John clearly did identify himself with Elijah (and Jesus identified him that way as well; see Matthew 11:14). It seems there may have been some speculation that the historical Elijah would literally return in a second coming; this is what John denied. Elijah would not come himself. Rather, one would come in his "spirit and power" and so fulfill Malachi's prophecy.
[23] Malachi 3:1

of Elijah's return. If we only had Malachi's prophecy to foretell the coming of a messenger *before* the Messiah, we might miss it.

Thankfully, Isaiah also speaks about a messenger to precede the return of Yahweh:

> "Comfort, comfort My people," says your God.
> "Speak tenderly to Jerusalem,
> And announce to her that her time of forced labor is over,
> Her iniquity has been pardoned,
> And she has received from the Lord's hand
> Double for all her sins."
> A voice of one crying out:
> Prepare the way of the Lord in the wilderness;
> Make a straight highway for our God in the desert.
> Every valley will be lifted up,
> And every mountain and hill will be leveled;
> The uneven ground will become smooth
> And the rough places, a plain.
> And the glory of the Lord will appear,
> And all humanity together will see it,
> For the mouth of the Lord has spoken.[24]

More than any other prophecy or type in the Bible, this passage lies at the heart of John's self-perception. When the Pharisees confronted him in John 1, they asked whether he was Elijah or another Old Testament prophet, supernaturally returned to the earth. John answered, "I am not." But when they continued to press him about his identity, he gave Isaiah 40 as his answer:

> He said, "I am the voice of one crying out in the

---
24 Isaiah 40:1–5

wilderness: Make straight the way of the Lord—just as Isaiah the prophet said."[25]

John's confident confession of his identity declared his beliefs about God, himself, and the times he lived in. He believed, in keeping with Isaiah 40:1–2, that the time for forgiveness of sins had come. That was the basis of his baptism "for the forgiveness of sins": somehow out there in the wilderness, he had come to know that God was *now* ending the rule of the curse and breaking the power of sin over his people by offering them forgiveness and restoration. He believed that his own existence and unique role in history had been foretold by Israel's greatest prophet hundreds of years before, and he believed that the Lord Yahweh himself was coming after him.

Furthermore, in some sense he believed the coming of Yahweh would be accomplished in and through the Messiah, whom he viewed as embodying God in some way, or at least as embodying God's purposes. In one breath he could say he had come to "prepare the way of Yahweh" and in the next, "I am not the Messiah, but I've been sent ahead of him."[26] John saw himself as a messenger preparing the way for *the* Messenger. He believed he was the herald of a king who was himself the herald—or personification—of Yahweh.

What John believed about himself is staggering to consider. And short of his being delusional, it's easy to see why it might take years of spiritual experience in a desert to make a man humble enough and clearsighted enough to accept such a calling and identity. While delusion can

---
25 John 1:23
26 John 3:28

accept the idea of personally being the second coming of one of the greatest men in history and the fulfillment of hundreds of years of prophecy, pride can't. Pride is too attached to control and self-determination. It takes a profound humility to surrender to a calling and identity like the one John carried. If you have ever wrestled with the calling of God on your own life, you know this: God's call can't be controlled or shaped according to our own preferences. In the end, it can only be submitted to.

John submitted to his. However those years in the desert played out, from the moment he reappeared in society as an adult of thirty or so years of age, John was like a man on fire. He ate locusts and wild honey; he dressed in camel skin. He was full of zeal and the Holy Spirit. He was a living reproach to the cultured refinement of the Herods and to those of his own Jewish people who valued their own comfort and worldly prosperity above the word of the Lord. When he called the religious leaders of his day "a brood of vipers" and thundered out, "Don't say to yourselves, 'We have Abraham for our father,' for God is able to raise up children of Abraham from these stones,"[27] everyone could feel in their bones the authority behind his words.

Releasing the Word of the Lord

When John reentered society as an adult, he announced that the kingdom of God was about to arrive and commanded everyone within earshot to repent and be baptized in recognition of this fact. He drew enormous

---

27 Matthew 3:9

crowds to the Jordan River, where he and his disciples baptized anyone who desired it and stirred up a lot of debate and trouble among the religious leaders of the time. Most people believed he was a prophet, although the religious establishment never officially got behind him or his message. The movement he started can fairly be called a revival.

John had a simple and arresting message:

> When he saw many of the Pharisees and Sadducees coming to the place of his baptism, he said to them, "Brood of vipers! Who warned you to flee from the coming wrath? Therefore produce fruit consistent with repentance. And don't presume to say to yourselves, 'We have Abraham as our father.' For I tell you that God is able to raise up children for Abraham from these stones! Even now the ax is ready to strike the root of the trees! Therefore, every tree that doesn't produce good fruit will be cut down and thrown into the fire.
>
> "I baptize you with water for repentance, but the One who is coming after me is more powerful than I. I am not worthy to remove His sandals. He Himself will baptize you with the Holy Spirit and fire. His winnowing shovel is in His hand, and He will clear His threshing floor and gather His wheat into the barn. But the chaff He will burn up with fire that never goes out."[28]

Later in Matthew 3, we're told that when Jesus arrived on the scene, he requested baptism from John. John initially refused, identifying Jesus as the one he had been

---

[28] Matthew 3:7–12

preaching about. But Jesus coaxed him into allowing it—and the act led to a dramatic experience for them both.

After Jesus was baptized, He went up immediately from the water. The heavens suddenly opened for Him, and He saw the Spirit of God descending like a dove and coming down on Him. And there came a voice from heaven:

> This is My beloved Son.
> I take delight in Him![29]

For John, the event was even more significant than it might have been for others, for one reason: God had already alerted him that this would happen and what it would mean. Shortly after, John pointed Jesus out publicly to others. The words he spoke in doing so were hardly an ordinary introduction. We might say they were John's statement of faith.

> The next day John saw Jesus coming toward him and said, "Here is the Lamb of God, who takes away the sin of the world! This is the One I told you about: 'After me comes a man who has surpassed me, because He existed before me.' I didn't know Him, but I came baptizing with water so He might be revealed to Israel."
>
> And John testified, "I watched the Spirit descending from heaven like a dove, and He rested on Him. I didn't know Him, but He who sent me to baptize with water told me, 'The One you see the Spirit descending and resting on—He is the One who baptizes with the Holy Spirit.' I have seen and testified that He is the Son of God!"[30]

---

[29] Matthew 3:16–17
[30] John 1:29–34

Fascinatingly, John's faith in—or perhaps I should say "faith about"—Jesus went far beyond what most people would have claimed about the Messiah in his day and age. Based on the passages we've read, we know John believed the time had come for Israel's long history of exile and oppression to end. He believed that Yahweh was about to return and deliver his people at long last. He believed Yahweh would do this through an individual, an "Anointed One" or Messiah who would rule as a king in the pattern of David and Solomon—as a victorious conqueror who loved the law of God and turned the people's hearts back to righteousness (in the mold of David); and as a supernaturally wise and just king reigning over a Golden Age of peace and prosperity (in the mold of Solomon).

And because of the prophecies regarding the curse, the monstrous empires, and the "little horn," John likely also believed that the Messiah's coming would be preceded by intense suffering. He may have believed this time of suffering had already passed, having taken place during the figurative 490 years between the Babylonian exile and his own day, or he may have seen it as still coming to a final head—perhaps even in his own sufferings.

So far, all of this was fairly standard. It was Messianic expectation that most faithful, biblically conservative Jews in the first century would have agreed on. John's contribution was timing—declaring that all these expectations were happening *now*. Yet, we also have some evidence that John believed Jesus was more than a man. In some sense, and more clearly than any prophet before him, he seems to have understood Jesus to be preexistent and divine. As we've already seen, in the first century AD there did exist a fringe belief in the Messiah as a divine being, probably derived from the visions of Daniel. John's own words strongly indicate he held to this much less normative belief. And he applied it to a man he could see standing in front of him—his own cousin.

> The next day John saw Jesus coming toward him and said, "Here is the Lamb of God, who takes away the sin of the world! This is the One I told you about: 'After me comes a man who has surpassed me, because He existed before me.' I didn't know Him, but I came baptizing with water so He might be revealed to Israel."[31]
>
> John responded, "No one can receive a single thing unless it's given to him from heaven. You yourselves can testify that I said, 'I am not the Messiah, but I've been sent ahead of Him.' He who has the bride is the groom. But the groom's friend, who stands by and listens for him, rejoices greatly at the groom's voice. So this joy of mine is complete. He must increase, but I must decrease ... The One who comes from above is above all. The one who is from the earth is earthly and speaks in earthly terms. The One who comes from heaven is above all."[32]

The Return of Ahab and Jezebel

The post-wilderness John was a recognized type in his own time and an almost incomprehensible one in ours. Even in his own day, though, he was controversial—and he made enemies. The Jewish religious leaders were afraid to confront him openly because of his gen-

---

31 John 1:29–31
32 John 3:27–31

eral popularity, but they were not the only people John rubbed the wrong way. He made a far more powerful enemy in the local king, Herod Antipas.

The Herods are regular villains in the gospels, beginning with Herod the Great, who ordered the killing of infants shortly after Jesus was born, and continuing on to Agrippa II, who heard Paul preach the gospel but failed to believe. Ethnically they were Idumeans, descendants of the ancient Edomites, who had been forcibly converted to Judaism a century before. The Herods were client kings of the Roman Empire, instated as kings of the Jews by Rome and sharing power over Judea with Roman governors. For the most part they were immoral, paranoid, and insecure, and the New Testament depicts them as regularly coming into conflict with the *true* king of the Jews and his followers—Jesus, his herald John the Baptist, and his later disciples.

According to the gospel of Mark, Herod had married his brother Philip's wife Herodias, and John—tactful as ever—publicly rebuked him for immorality. At this point, the story takes on eerie echoes of Elijah's ongoing antagonism with Ahab and Jezebel—Herodias developed a grudge, much like Jezebel had done with Elijah centuries before, and applied pressure to her husband over it. This combined with Herod's weakness and paranoia over possible insurrection, strongly reminiscent of Ahab's vacillating personality, led to him arresting John and throwing him in prison.

That is where John was, in fact, when he developed doubt, owned up to it, and sent his disciples to Jesus to ask whether he really was the Messiah or not.

In the Shadow of the Christ

Even with all these background details in place, John the Baptist remains an enigmatic figure. We know little about his life, and we have only a few highlights from his messages. Although he started a movement of revival and repentance that galvanized Galilee and Judea, earned him the enmity of the local political powers, shook the religious establishment, and even managed to spread around the world,[33] he remains in shadow—eclipsed, as he said he would and should be, by Jesus.

But all of this, what we know about John and what we don't, leads to an inescapable realization: When it came to Jesus's identity as "the Messiah" or "not the Messiah," John had more than a dog in the fight. *His entire identity rested on being right about Jesus.* He was the messenger of Yahweh and the preparer of a nation for the Messiah, whom John believed had come at last. It was *John* who used all the respect and authority given to him as the leader of a mass revival movement to launch Jesus into ministry by publicly declaring him to be the preexistent Messiah—the "Lamb of God, who takes away the sins of the world," the "Son of God," and the

---

[33] A little over twenty years later, Paul in his missionary travels encountered devotees of John's message in Ephesus, a Greek city in Asia Minor some 1200 miles from Judea. Earlier in the same city, Paul's coworkers Priscilla and Aquila heard a gifted preacher named Apollos preaching "John's baptism" in the local synagogue, and they pulled him aside, updated him on the events in Judea after John's ministry had ended, and converted him to Christ. Apparently John's message, "Repent for the kingdom is at hand," reached many people around the world and prepared them for the message of Jesus's messiahship, resurrection, and ascension to the throne of heaven—the message, in other words, that in Jesus, the kingdom of God had come.

"Bridegroom," to whom the Bride, the purified remnant of Israel, rightly belonged. It was John who said that the Spirit had descended from heaven and identified Jesus as the heavenly man. It was John who moved many to believe.

And yet, at the end of this journey to rock-solid convictions and beliefs that would be insane if they weren't true, we arrive at John's question in Matthew 11:

"Are you the One who is to come, or should we expect someone else?"

Bitter and blunt, his question is an admission of potential failure on his own part and an accusation of misrepresentation on Jesus's.

The question also contains a barely veiled threat. Because it was asked in public, while Jesus was actively ministering to the crowds, it was meant to catalyze a response not only from Jesus but from the crowds. If Jesus didn't answer satisfactorily, the crowds should feel free to go elsewhere.[34]

For us too, doubt can be so awful and so destructive precisely because it hits at our identity. If we have really believed, or we've thought we have, then we have built an identity around that belief. We don't just "believe in Jesus"; we *are* Christians, or Jesus freaks, or Presbyterians, or Catholics, or whatever our particular lane may be. We have participated in community centered on our beliefs. We have seen ourselves through faith's lens.

---

[34] I owe this insight to Robert L. Deffinbaugh, "John's Problem with Jesus (Luke 7:18–35)." Published at Bible.org, bible.org/seriespage/22-johns-problem-jesus-luke-718-35.

When we doubt, it's not just an intellectual exercise. It rocks our sense of what the world is and most of all, of *who we are.*

John's question is painful for us too.

We thought You were the One. We built our lives on it. But ...

"Should we expect someone else?"

THE GREATEST BORN OF WOMEN

If John had hoped to force Jesus to reveal himself, he was disappointed. Jesus's answer, which we will explore in more depth in the next chapter, gave John very good reasons to keep hanging in there, but it did not definitively answer his question (or, by extension, the question of the crowds). Jesus simply quoted Isaiah 61:1:

> Jesus replied to [John's disciples], "Go and report to John what you hear and see: the blind see, the lame walk, those with skin diseases are healed, the deaf hear, the dead are raised, and the poor are told the good news."
>
> He then tacked on a curious charge: "And if anyone is not offended because of Me, he is blessed."[35]

Having publicly answered John's question, however, Jesus then turned to the crowds. His next words were quite defensive—but not on behalf of himself or his mission. He became defensive of *John*. John, after all, had publicly exposed his vulnerability and weakness, and Jesus had his back. He made sure that in the eyes of ev-

---

35 Matthew 11:4–6

eryone present, his cousin's honor remained fully intact. At the same time, he offered more mysterious insight on the historical significance of his own ministry and that of John:

> As these men went away, Jesus began to speak to the crowds about John: "What did you go out into the wilderness to see? A reed swaying in the wind? What then did you go out to see? A man dressed in soft clothes? Look, those who wear soft clothes are in kings' palaces. But what did you go out to see? A prophet? Yes, I tell you, and far more than a prophet. This is the one it is written about:
>
>> Look, I am sending My messenger ahead of You;
>> he will prepare Your way before You.
>
>> "I assure you: Among those born of women no one greater than John the Baptist has appeared, but the least in the kingdom of heaven is greater than he. From the days of John the Baptist until now, the kingdom of heaven has been suffering violence, and the violent have been seizing it by force. For all the prophets and the Law prophesied until John; if you're willing to accept it, he is the Elijah who is to come. Anyone who has ears should listen!"[36]

The messenger of Malachi present and accounted for. Children of the kingdom of heaven, whose greatness somehow eclipses that of the greatest of the prophets. The *end* of the law and prophets. Violence taking the kingdom by force. Elijah arrived, but imprisoned and doubting—and declared by an apparent Messiah who refuses to declare himself.

---

36 Matthew 11:7–15

All of these strange and enigmatic concepts are a clue as to where John's expectations may have begun to go awry. Although he had a clearer understanding of Jesus's identity and mission than any prophet before him had ever had, the story of the Messiah as it actually began to unfold in the real world still challenged him with its unexpected shape.

It may challenge us too. And so it is to that unexpected shape that we now turn.

Chapter 7:
The Bend in the Road: When Everything Goes Sideways

We've journeyed together now through John the Baptist's understanding of the Scriptures. We've come to an understanding, as best as we are able from such a distance in time, of the content of his faith. We know what he expected from Jesus and how he understood his own role and identity in the plan of God.

So why, two years into Jesus's ministry, did John reach a place where he was no longer convinced that he had correctly identified the Messiah?

It's a pertinent question. Although it's common in Christian circles to explain defections by saying that if someone has fallen away, they must not have really believed (or really "been saved") in the first place, I think this treads on dangerous ground not only because it leads us to judging the hearts of others but also because it may lead us to interpret our own doubts in unhelpful ways. Most of us are *really convinced* of the things we believe, whether that's because of study or personal experience or because we've simply never really questioned what we were taught. And yet life can move any one of us away from that rock-solid certainty. It happened to John, whom Jesus called "more than a prophet" and "the greatest among those born of women." It can certainly happen to us.

For some of us, it happens because of a crisis. A prayer doesn't get answered. Someone dies, and in our grief and anger we can't see any way to hang onto faith. A scandal rocks our church or takes down a Christian leader we have looked up to and followed, and it casts everything they taught—and we believed—into question. "Offenses must come," Jesus said in Matthew 18:7, employing a Greek word that means most literally "a stumbling block" or a "snare"—in other words, that which causes someone to become entrapped or to stumble along his way. "But woe to that man by whom the offense comes." Earlier, in verse 6 he said, "Whoever causes the downfall of one of these little ones who believe in Me—it would be better for him if a heavy millstone were hung around his neck and he were drowned in the depths of the sea!"

For many, it happens more quietly. Questions that have festered for years simply become too loud and too settled for us to ignore any longer. In many cases, it comes as a result of a simple environmental change: a student who has always been a "strong Christian" goes off to college, makes a new set of (nonbelieving) friends, is exposed to a suite of secular thinking and pluralistic worldviews, and simply finds he or she does not believe anymore. Perhaps we discover that some fundamental underpinning of our belief system is shakier than we believed it to be or is even simply wrong. Or perhaps we rebel against an aspect of the particular Christian *culture* we grew up in—its unique rules, dress standards, or gender prescriptions, for example. In all those cases we might be in danger of throwing the proverbial baby out with the bathwater.

In the case of John the Baptist, we can't know what precisely prompted his crisis of faith. The Bible doesn't tell us, and we don't have access to the thoughts and feelings of a man who lived two thousand years ago. But we can make educated guesses, based on what we now know about the Old Testament prophecies and the Messianic expectations that had developed by John's time.

Somehow, Jesus had let John down—or at least, John thought he had. If we've ever felt the same way, it may be instructive to figure out how.

The Life of Jesus and Reasons for Doubt

First of all, there was Jesus's astonishingly nonmilitant character. Of course, people in Jesus's day might have been waiting for him to suddenly change tack, take up the sword, and start a military revolution—phase two of his ministry, after all the healing and teaching and miracles to attest that he had been sent from God and enable him to build a following. But two years in, Jesus showed no sign that he ever intended to do that.

Even worse, he'd recently begun to say some extremely pessimistic, almost nihilistic things; and it's fair to assume John's disciples had carried word of this to John in prison. To the best of your ability, listen to these words of Jesus, conveyed during his commissioning of his apostles in chapter 10, with the ears of a first-century Jew waiting for the Son of David to be revealed. For that matter, listen with the ears of John the Baptist, having given your whole life for this cause!

> Don't assume that I came to bring peace on the earth. I did not come to bring peace, but a sword. For I came to turn
>
> > a man against his father,
> > a daughter against her mother,
> > a daughter-in-law against her mother-in-law;
> > and a man's enemies will be
> > the members of his household.
>
> The person who loves father or mother more than Me is not worthy of Me; the person who loves son or daughter more than Me is not worthy of Me. *And whoever doesn't take up his cross and follow Me is not worthy of Me. Anyone finding his life will lose it, and anyone losing his life because of Me will find it.*[1]

Remember that while the Jews did expect Jesus to "take up a sword," they thought he would do it in order to bring and enforce peace. The goal was supposed to be victory, not defeat. *And no one in the first century carried crosses except people who intended to die on them.*

This was not a cheery prospect. N.T. Wright reminds us:

> The point is often made but bears repetition: we in the modern West, who wear jeweled crosses around our

---
1 Matthew 10:34–39, my emphasis.

necks, stamp them on Bibles and prayer books, and carry them in cheerful processions, need regularly to be reminded that the very word "cross" was a word you would most likely not utter in polite society. The thought of it would not only put you off your dinner; it could give you sleepless nights. And if you had actually seen a crucifixion or two, as many in the Roman world would have, your sleep itself would have been invaded by nightmares as the memories came flooding back unbidden, memories of humans half alive and half dead, lingering on perhaps for days on end, covered in blood and flies, nibbled by rats, pecked at by crows, with weeping but helpless relatives still keeping watch, and with hostile or mocking crowds adding their insults to the terrible injuries.

Crucifixion was, simply put, "the lowest point possible for a human being."[2] It was also terribly familiar. The Romans used crucifixion to destroy, demoralize, and humiliate their enemies, especially those who rebelled against them. So Roman provinces like Palestine lived in the shadow of the cross. In Galilee, a major revolt had taken place just four years before John was born,[3] and it ended with the public crucifixion of two thousand Jewish rebels. John's father and mother would have remembered that—talked about it. His older cousins would have suffered posttraumatic nightmares, recalling what they saw as children. Neither Jesus nor John could afford to hold a romanticized idea of martyrdom, especially through crucifixion. They, their friends and their families knew the specter of the cross too well.

---

2 N.T. Wright, *The Day the Revolution Began* (NY: HarperOne, 2016), 54–55
3 Ibid., 58.

This being the case, if Jesus was telling his followers to expect to be crucified, it seemed he expected his mission to fail. Remember, too, that Daniel had spoken of a period of extreme suffering before the kingdom of God came—a time when the "Little Horn" would wear out the saints and nearly defeat them. Jesus's talk of crosses and death—*"losing your life in order to find it"*—may have led to John to wonder if Jesus was simply bringing this period to a head. Perhaps Jesus's life was meant to be the apex of Israelite suffering before the Messiah's coming. But if Jesus died, taking his followers down with him, he could not *be* the Messiah. A dead man, murdered by Rome in the most degrading and horrible way possible, could not be the Son of David who would defeat Rome, take the throne, and restore the prosperity of Israel.

Compounding all of this confusion was Jesus's somewhat unusual relationship to the law and to the idea of Jewish holiness (or "set-apartness") in general. As Jesus himself pointed out, he was not an ascetic like John, and many (especially the Pharisees) saw him as overly friendly with those Jews who compromised the law, embracing Greek and Roman culture and therefore (in their minds) pushing the Jewish people toward unfaithfulness to God. The usual parlance for Jews who did these things was "tax collectors and sinners," and Jesus was famous for associating with them on friendly, nonconfrontational terms.

> For John came neither eating nor drinking, and they say, "He has a demon." The Son of Man came eating and drinking, and they say, "Here is a glutton and a drunkard, a friend of tax collectors and sinners."[4]

---

4 Matthew 11:18–19

John's Question, Jesus's Answer

By now it should be clear that two years into his ministry, Jesus was failing to live up to John's expectations of the Messiah. Remember, those expectations did not come out of thin air. They came out of a deep grasp of Scripture and the plans of God. They came out of a powerful personal faith. John trusted God, and he *knew* what God's Messiah—his Anointed One—was supposed to be and do. And those expectations had shaped John's identity too. In many ways, he was the person he was because of his faith in God to act, in his lifetime, in the way he expected.

When Jesus first came on the scene, John was certain he'd found the One. After all, he personally saw the Holy Spirit come out of heaven like a dove and rest on Jesus. He heard the voice of God thunder out of heaven, "This is my beloved Son." Remember Psalm 2?

> I will declare the Lord's decree:
> He said to Me, "You are My Son;
> today I have become Your Father.
> Ask of Me,
> and I will make the nations Your inheritance
> and the ends of the earth Your possession.
> You will break them with a rod of iron;
> You will shatter them like pottery."[5]

But as time passed, Jesus began to look less and less like the one John was waiting for. So John pushed the issue. He forced the question. He needed to know; the people needed to know.

---

5 Psalm 2:7–9

And *this* was Jesus's answer. We've read it before, but let's read it again—this time with all the Old Testament prophecy we've read still at the forefront of our minds:

> Jesus replied to them, "Go and report to John what you hear and see: the blind see, the lame walk, those with skin diseases are healed, the deaf hear, the dead are raised, and the poor are told the good news. And if anyone is not offended because of Me, he is blessed."[6]

Initially this doesn't look like an answer at all. And in one sense, it's not. Jesus could have said "Yes," or "No," which is what John apparently wanted him to say. Instead he offered a riddle. But the riddle does have a fairly clear inference. The passage Jesus quoted here is Isaiah 61. And of course, there's more to it than what he quoted. Actually, *all* of Isaiah 61 is important, but let's zoom in on its first three verses:

> The Spirit of the Lord God is on Me,
> because the Lord has anointed Me
> to bring good news to the poor.
> He has sent Me to heal the brokenhearted,
> to proclaim liberty to the captives
> and freedom to the prisoners;
> to proclaim the year of the Lord's favor,
> and the day of our God's vengeance;
> to comfort all who mourn,
> to provide for those who mourn in Zion;
> to give them a crown of beauty instead of ashes,
> festive oil instead of mourning,
> and splendid clothes instead of despair.

---

[6] Matthew 11:4–6

> And they will be called righteous trees,
> planted by the Lord
> to glorify Him.

To the crowds, Jesus only quotes the part of the passage that highlights the works of healing, proclamation, and deliverance. *These things are being done,* he's pointing out. The captives go free. The poor hear the gospel preached to them. But John knows the Scriptures. So do his disciples; so do many of the people in the crowds. So they know the *identity* that goes with those works, and they know the *year* that goes with those works.

The identity is Messianic: "The Spirit of the Lord God is on Me, because the Lord has anointed Me."

(Again, for John, those words must have reminded him of his own vision; he personally *saw* the Holy Spirit come upon Jesus.)

The year is the Jubilee. It is the "year of the Lord's favor"—of Yahweh's forgiveness and grace, and of his vengeance upon his enemies. The word translated "liberty" here, Hebrew *deror*, is not the usual word meaning "freedom." It's the word used in Leviticus and elsewhere specifically to speak of the Jubilee release.[7] If John is willing to put two and two together, Jesus is telling him: *My works will tell you who I am and what is happening. I am the Messiah, and the time of the kingdom has come.* John was presumably among those who believed the 490 years of Daniel were ending in his time. The effect of Jesus's words was to say: *You are right.*

---

[7] See "1865. deror," *Strong's Concordance*. Hosted at BibleHub.com. Cf. *Brown-Driver-Briggs Hebrew and English Lexicon,* Unabridged, Electronic Database. Copyright © 2002, 2003, 2006 by Biblesoft, Inc.

So why, we might wonder, was Jesus so oblique about it? Why not come right out and just say "Yes, I am the Messiah"? (We might wonder the same thing about our own doubts sometimes. *Why are you so hard to pin down? Why don't you just answer me? Why don't you just show up and make this obvious?*)

After all, knowing all the background, you can easily read Jesus's answer and see that he's claiming to be the Messiah.

On the other hand, if you want to, you can easily read it and say he's not claiming any such thing.

It's a deliberately evasive answer.

The pragmatic reason Jesus would answer like this may be that he lived in a revolutionary hotbed where declaring oneself to be the Messiah would bring serious problems with the ruling authorities *and* with those of his own countrymen who had an agenda for just what the Messiah should do, when, where, and with whom. But the pragmatic answer has a spiritual side too, an incredibly relevant side for all of us. You see, the reason some of Jesus's countrymen had an agenda he needed to avoid was *not* that they didn't know the Scripture or trust in God. They did, on both counts. It was that, through no fault of their own, they had gotten the story wrong.

John had gotten the story wrong.

Even though it was based in the Scriptures.

Even though he could have read his version of events right off the pages of Isaiah, David, and Daniel.

Even though he was a man full of faith and the Holy Spirit, walking out a life of radical obedience, doing *exactly* what he was supposed to do.

He still had the story wrong. He was missing pieces, and he didn't know it. As the saying goes, he didn't know what he didn't know. Or as the book of Job puts it, *That which I see not, teach Thou me.*[8]

So Jesus, with his oblique, frustrating, easily misinterpreted non-answer that *was* in fact an answer, was calling John to do something radical. On the one hand, he was challenging him, through his clear allusion to the Messiah and the Jubilee in Isaiah 61, to renew his faith. *Yes, John, I am the Anointed One. No, you didn't get it wrong. Yes, the time has come. The kingdom is here. Take all this up and believe it again.*

But on the other hand, he was calling him to be willing to *not* understand for a moment, to lay down his old certainties, and to step into a bigger story. He was asking John to realize that as much as he had the bones right, he might have had the body wrong.

In our doubts, we too have a choice to make. We can question God. (We should question God—actively, in prayer, and to his face.) But we can also, and *should* also, question ourselves. If and when we feel that God has let us down, that he is defaulting on his promises and failing to come through in the way we rightly expected, we can step back and reexamine the story.

It's just possible there's something we're missing.

---

[8] Job 34:32, KJV

Chapter 8:
The Gospel That Subverts Expectations

More than thirty years after John's conversation with Jesus—thirty years after John's death, when the crucifixion and resurrection of Jesus were in the past and the "good news preached to the poor" had taken on contours previously unimaginable—a former Pharisee named Paul wrote to a fledgling community of believers in Jesus Christ. Or, as the name literally means, "Jesus the Messiah."

> God's administration ... was given to me for you, to make God's message fully known, *the mystery hidden for ages and generations but now revealed to His saints.* God wanted to make known among the Gentiles the glorious wealth *of this mystery,* which is Christ in you, the hope of glory.[1]

To another such community, this one in the city of Ephesus, he wrote again about the mystery now revealed:

> This grace was given to me—the least of all the

---
[1] Colossians 1:25b–27, my emphasis

saints—to proclaim to the Gentiles the incalculable riches of the Messiah, and to shed light for all about the administration of the mystery hidden for ages in God who created all things.[2]

And finally, to the church in Corinth:

We do speak a wisdom among the mature, but not a wisdom of this age, or of the rulers of this age, who are coming to nothing. On the contrary, we speak *God's hidden wisdom in a mystery*, a wisdom God predestined before the ages for our glory. None of the rulers of this age knew this wisdom, for if they had known it, they would not have crucified the Lord of glory. But as it is written:

What eye did not see and ear did not hear,
and what never entered the human mind—
God prepared this for those who love Him.[3]

For Paul, whose life message was to spread the word of Christ and his kingdom, "God's hidden wisdom in a mystery" was a favorite theme. This was because in his own day, he had seen the mystery revealed.

All along, there had been a plan and a story in the heart of God—a wisdom hidden in the Scriptures and in the actions of God throughout history. Yet it wasn't until Jesus lived it out that anyone could see it for what it was.

Throughout the New Testament, Paul is a mirror image to John the Baptist—a reversed reflection. John was straining forward, trying to see the future in light

---

[2] Ephesians 3:8–11
[3] 1 Corinthians 2:6–9, my emphasis

of past revelation. Paul, on the other hand, stood in the light of new revelation and with it, understood the past for the first time.

One of the passages Paul may have been alluding to in 1 Corinthians 2 is this one, from Isaiah 64:

> When You did awesome works
> that we did not expect,
> You came down,
> and the mountains quaked at Your presence.
> From ancient times no one has heard,
> no one has listened,
> no eye has seen any God except You,
> who acts on behalf of the one who waits for Him.[4]

Despite all of their expectations, there was a side to the gospel of the kingdom that Israel had never seen. And yet, it had been there all along.

THE SONG OF THE SUFFERING SERVANT

Back in the book of Isaiah, four poetic passages have been identified by scholars as "the Servant Songs." Each speaks of someone called "God's Servant." At times the Servant himself speaks; at other times, God speaks about him. Whoever or whatever the Servant is, he is clearly central to the plans of God in the future. We meet him first in Isaiah 42, which begins:

---

[4] Isaiah 64:3–4. The wording of the King James Bible, reflecting an alternate possible translation, may sound more familiar to readers of the New Testament: "For since the beginning of the world men have not heard, nor perceived by the ear, neither hath the eye seen, O God, beside thee, what he hath prepared for him that waiteth for him."

> "This is My Servant; I strengthen Him,
> this is My Chosen One; I delight in Him.
> I have put My Spirit on Him;
> He will bring justice to the nations.
> He will not cry out or shout
> or make His voice heard in the streets.
> He will not break a bruised reed,
> and He will not put out a smoldering wick;
> He will faithfully bring justice.
> He will not grow weak or be discouraged
> until He has established justice on earth.
> The islands will wait for His instruction."
> This is what God, Yahweh, says—
> who created the heavens and stretched them out,
> who spread out the earth and what comes from it,
> who gives breath to the people on it
> and life to those who walk on it—
> "I, Yahweh, have called You
> for a righteous purpose,
> and I will hold You by Your hand.
> I will keep You and appoint You
> to be a covenant for the people
> and a light to the nations,
> in order to open blind eyes,
> to bring out prisoners from the dungeon,
> and those sitting in darkness from the prison house.
> I am Yahweh, that is My name;
> I will not give My glory to another
> or My praise to idols.[5]

Much like Daniel 7 and 9, the Servant Songs are no-

---

5 Isaiah 42:1–8

toriously tricky. Found in Isaiah 42:1–9, Isaiah 49:1–12, Isaiah 50:4–9, and Isaiah 52:13–53:12, they seem at times to speak of Israel as a nation—a corporate entity personified, much like the Son of Man in Daniel 7 who represents all the "holy ones" of God. At other times, they seem to speak of a single man. Perhaps, some speculated, the Servant was Isaiah—indeed, this was the question asked by the Ethiopian eunuch in Acts 8, when Jesus's follower Philip met him in his chariot reading from a scroll of Isaiah. "I ask you," the eunuch asked, "who is the prophet saying this about—himself or another person?"[6] Of course, Philip explained that the passage was speaking about Jesus. But that's getting way ahead of our story.

Or perhaps, some speculated, if the Servant is a representative of the nation, he is also a king. N.T. Wright agrees that the set of songs "carries at the least overtones of the 'royal' passages in the first part of the book ... There is a well-known fluidity between the nation and its royal representative: the king holds the key to the destiny of the people."[7]

King or not, prophet or not, it would be tempting within the surrounding context of Isaiah to identify the Servant with the Messiah. This is true for exactly the same reason that it's tempting to see the Son of Man not *only* as representing the people of God but *also* as being a Messianic figure: the Scriptures seem to indicate both.

---

[6] Acts 8:34
[7] N.T. Wright, *The Day the Revolution Began* (New York: HarperOne, 2016), 139

When we meet the Servant for the second time, in Isaiah 49, he is clearly identified as Israel:

> The Lord called me before I was born.
> He named me while I was in my mother's womb.
> He made my words like a sharp sword;
> He hid me in the shadow of His hand.
> He made me like a sharpened arrow;
> He hid me in His quiver.
> *He said to me, "You are My Servant, Israel;*
> I will be glorified in him."[8]

But only one verse later, he is not Israel but rather an individual whose task is to bring Israel back to God and indeed, even reach out to the nations with Yahweh's glorious light:

> And now, says the Lord,
> who formed me from the womb to be His Servant,
> to bring Jacob back to Him
> so that Israel might be gathered to Him;
> for I am honored in the sight of the Lord,
> and my God is my strength—
> He says,
> "It is not enough for you to be My Servant
> raising up the tribes of Jacob
> and restoring the protected ones of Israel.
> I will also make you a light for the nations,
> to be My salvation to the ends of the earth."[9]

So far, so good—from these beautiful passages, we would be forgiven for assuming the Servant was one and the same with the Anointed One, the prophesied Mes-

---

8 Isaiah 49:1b–3, my emphasis
9 Isaiah 49:5–6

siah who would come and rule as king, ushering in the Messianic Age and the kingdom of God on earth. But this poem, the second Servant Song, isn't over. Immediately after this promise of salvation and light comes a surprising passage, one that begins to build a case *against* this figure as being the Messiah after all.

It says:

> This is what the Lord,
> the Redeemer of Israel, his Holy One, says
> to one who is despised,
> to one abhorred by people,
> to a servant of rulers:
> "Kings will see and stand up,
> and princes will bow down,
> because of the Lord, who is faithful,
> the Holy One of Israel—and He has chosen you."[10]

This new theme, of the Servant as someone who is despised and abhorred—some translations say "despised and rejected"—is new. And it's decidedly non-Messianic. Remember how Isaiah has described the Messianic King before now! Remember the psalms of David and the triumphant victories of Zephaniah and Micah. Whoever this Servant was—prophet, king, or simply prophetic representation of Israel—he could not be the same as the one destined to rule an eternal kingdom, subjecting all the nations to his power and authority.

If you think I'm making too much out of one little phrase about abhorrence and rejection, that would prob-

---

[10] Isaiah 49:7

ably be a fair point—if Isaiah 49 were all we had to go on. But two more Servant Songs remain, and in them, things get worse. Much worse. Isaiah 50 begins with a typical description of the Servant as faithfully receiving the word of God and serving others with it, but then comes this note of suffering again:

> The Lord God has opened My ear,
> and I was not rebellious;
> I did not turn back.
> I gave My back to those who beat Me,
> and My cheeks to those who tore out My beard.
> I did not hide My face from scorn and spitting.[11]

And finally we reach the climactic Servant Song, starting in Isaiah 52:13 and carrying through to the end of Isaiah 53. This time the horror bears down relentlessly:

> See, My Servant will act wisely;
> He will be raised and lifted up and greatly exalted.
> Just as many were appalled at You—
> His appearance was so disfigured
> that He did not look like a man,
> and His form did not resemble a human being—
> so He will sprinkle many nations.
> Kings will shut their mouths because of Him,
> For they will see what had not been told them,
> and they will understand what they had not heard.[12]

Isaiah 53 goes on to describe someone who suffers terribly, silently undergoing oppression and affliction "like a lamb led to the slaughter." In some way, the chapter indicates, this suffering would be vicarious, endured

---

11 Isaiah 50:5–6
12 Isaiah 52:13–15

on behalf of the nation of Israel and because of Israel's sins. And it would be final. The Servant would not just suffer—he would die.

> He was taken away because of oppression and judgment;
> and who considered His fate?
> For He was cut off from the land of the living;
> He was struck because of my people's rebellion.
> They made His grave with the wicked
> and with a rich man at His death,
> although He had done no violence
> and had not spoken deceitfully.[13]

And yet somehow, even through his death, the Servant would be vindicated and would help to bring about the redemption of the people. "By His hand," Isaiah wrote in verse 10, "the Lord's pleasure will be accomplished."

The songs are a mystery. Like the Servant himself, their true meaning was "hidden in the shadow of the Lord's hand." And so they engendered debate for centuries.

One thing did seem clear, however: the Servant *was* Israel, as Isaiah 49:7 clearly says. Israel, after all, had been chosen and called by God for a purpose. They were supposed to be the nation among whom Yahweh dwelled on earth. Their promised land was intended to be the place where his kingdom was manifest and the nations came to be blessed. The Servant Songs indicate God had not forgotten his plan for them.

Of course, in their rebellion against God, they had

---

[13] Isaiah 53:8–9

temporarily faltered and failed in their mission. Another passage in Isaiah laments the downfall of those who worship deaf and dumb idols and like them, lose their spiritual senses:[14]

> "Listen, you deaf!
> Look, you blind, so that you may see.
> Who is blind but My servant,
> or deaf like My messenger I am sending?
> Who is blind like My dedicated one,
> or blind like the servant of the Lord?
> Though seeing many things, you do not obey.
> Though his ears are open, he does not listen."[15]

But even in their blind-and-deaf disobedience and apostasy, God would not relinquish his claim on Israel or revoke his calling on them as a nation. They would still be the Servant of the Lord. And because of their sins, which gave death and destruction power over them just as sin always does, they would suffer immensely—just as the curse had promised; just as the prophets foretold; just as Daniel saw in his apocalyptic visions.

Despite their failures, the Servant of Isaiah's four mysterious songs was clearly Israel. A second popular interpretation, however, held that it was not *all* Israel who were called the Lord's Servant in these passages, but only a faithful and devout remnant—a small group of righteous worshipers who would suffer, yet ultimately

---

14 G.K. Beale has written at length on this insight. See G.K. Beale, *We Become What We Worship: A Biblical Theology of Idolatry* (Downers Grove, IL: IVP Academic, 2008).
15 Isaiah 42:18–20

be vindicated. In the end, after and somehow *through* their suffering, redemption would come.

The Mystery Revealed

Two thousand years after Jesus, of course, we read Isaiah 53 and see no mystery at all. We immediately blurt out, "Oh, that's talking about Jesus on the cross." *It's obvious.*

But it wasn't.

There was no clear, obvious, logical prophecy in the Old Testament proclaiming that the *Messiah,* the anointed Son of David, Savior and Ruler of the World, would suffer and die. There was no clear, obvious, logical prophecy that said *after* he suffered and died, he would be raised back to life and ascend into heaven.

There was nothing like the story we tell now, the story we call the gospel—the story lived out by Jesus, the Galilean cousin of John the Baptist.

Yes, it was all there. After all, in the light of Jesus, who could read Isaiah 53 in any other way?

> Yet He Himself bore our sicknesses,
> and He carried our pains;
> but we in turn regarded Him stricken,
> struck down by God, and afflicted.
> But He was pierced because of our transgressions,
> crushed because of our iniquities;
> punishment for our peace was on Him,
> and we are healed by His wounds.
> We all went astray like sheep;
> we all have turned to our own way;

[and the Lord has laid on Him
the iniquity of us all.][16]
He was oppressed and afflicted,
yet He did not open His mouth.
Like a lamb led to the slaughter
and like a sheep silent before her shearers,
He did not open His mouth.
He was taken away because of oppression and judgment;
and who considered His fate?
For He was cut off from the land of the living;
He was struck because of my people's rebellion.
They made His grave with the wicked
and with a rich man at His death,
although He had done no violence
and had not spoken deceitfully.
Yet the Lord was pleased to crush Him severely.
When You make Him a restitution offering,
He will see His seed, He will prolong His days,
and by His hand, the Lord's pleasure will be accomplished.
He will see it out of His anguish,
and He will be satisfied with His knowledge.
My righteous Servant will justify many,
and He will carry their iniquities.
Therefore I will give Him the many as a portion,
and He will receive the mighty as spoil,
because He submitted Himself to death,
and was counted among the rebels;

---

16 The bracketed text is given in the ESV rather than the HCSB. The Holman text reads "And the LORD has punished Him for the iniquity of us all." The ESV is more literal, and I think the different implication is important. The footnotes for the NASB, one of the most literal of English translations, renders it "the LORD has caused the iniquity of us all to encounter Him."

> yet He bore the sin of many
> and interceded for the rebels.[17]

But this wasn't the story people in Jesus's day thought the Bible was telling. It had *never* been the story they thought it told. Before the cross and resurrection—who would have ever put this together? Even Paul the Pharisee didn't see it, assuming the resurrection was a big hoax until the risen Jesus met him on the road to Damascus and knocked him to the ground with the blinding light of his glory. (*I will make you a light to the nations,* Isaiah said. *I am sending you to the nations,* Jesus told Paul—after quite literally blinding him, temporarily, with his light. *I am the light of the world.*)

So here it is: this was not the story John the Baptist saw.

His faith, formed, informed, and infilled by the content of the Scriptures, had no conception of *this* story.

John understood suffering. Of course he did. He'd spent his life in the wilderness embracing suffering. He was suffering *now*. He sent his question to Jesus from a cold, narrow prison cell. He sent his question to Jesus with an axe hanging over his head. "Are you the one, or should we look for another?" *Have the sorrows and sufferings of Israel reached their end, or are you just one more in a long line of prophets who will face martyrdom without bringing the kingdom?*

Not surprisingly, Daniel had seen a glimpse of all this too. And also not surprisingly, no one had understood it.

---

[17] Isaiah 53:4–12

> *Know and understand this …*
> *After those 62 weeks*
> *the Messiah will be cut off*
> *and will have nothing.*
> *The people of the coming prince*
> *will destroy the city and the sanctuary.*
> *The end will come with a flood,*
> *and until the end there will be war;*
> *desolations are decreed.*

With all of this background, Jesus's follow-up to the crowd is all the more poignant.

As these men went away, Jesus began to speak to the crowds about John: "What did you go out into the wilderness to see? A reed swaying in the wind? What then did you go out to see? A man dressed in soft clothes? Look, those who wear soft clothes are in kings' palaces. But what did you go out to see? A prophet? Yes, I tell you, and far more than a prophet. This is the one it is written about:

> Look, I am sending My messenger ahead of You;
> he will prepare Your way before You.

"I assure you: Among those born of women no one greater than John the Baptist has appeared, but the least in the kingdom of heaven is greater than he. From the days of John the Baptist until now, the kingdom of heaven has been suffering violence, and the violent have been seizing it by force. For all the prophets and the Law prophesied until John; if you're willing to accept it, he is the Elijah who is to come. Anyone who has ears should listen!"[18]

---

18 Matthew 11:7–15

Jesus's answer was clear. The crowds with their limited understanding would never be able to call the tune properly. God's prophets, and ultimately God's Messianic king, would sing a different song. And although these early forerunners of the kingdom appeared to be confronted and even overtaken by violence, even though it looked as though the end had come, appearances would prove deceiving. In fact, Jesus told the crowds, the kingdom—afflicted and suffering violence—truly was at hand. John truly was Elijah. Prophecy was playing out before their eyes, even though it looked incredibly different from what they had anticipated.

Ultimately, the whole story would hang together. To see it, the people needed only to stay in faith—to *remain in his love*—long enough to learn how the pieces fit.

WHAT ARE *YOU* LOOKING FOR?

Having answered John's question, Jesus turned to the crowds and challenged them too. Essentially he asked them, "What are *you* looking for? Why are you here? Are you looking for answers, or did you just come to see a spectacle? Are you looking for the Messiah? Did you see Elijah when you looked at John—or just a ringmaster in a circus?"

The question is pertinent to all of us. It's easy to gather around Jesus just because that's what everyone else we know is doing. It's easy to be drawn by the activity, by the lights, by the music, or by the miracles. Not everyone has the earnest involvement and investment of a John the Baptist, although some of us do. So Jesus challenges us all: *Why are we here?*

Why have we come to God? Why have we stuck with him? Are we looking for a miracle? A comfortable morality? A simple path to fit in with our family and friends? Are we looking for pat answers? Do we want prosperity, a blessing, some kind of guarantee? Is it about a ticket to heaven, or about a sense of surety in our souls, or about feeling good about ourselves—feeling secure, feeling smug? *Why are we here?* Why did we come? Are we looking to fill our hunger? Are we seeking something transcendent? Did we sense—do we sense—that our need for love, for purpose, or for fulfillment may find its answer here? Are we answering a tug deep in our spirits, deep calling unto deep? Are we pushing our questions to the limit? Have we come seeking something greater than ourselves—something we can fall down and worship?

Why are we here?

Then Jesus went on. He knew, of course, that when they left this place and this encounter, the people would talk about what they had heard. They would gossip and speculate. They would have opinions, about Jesus and about John. That's human nature, after all. But Jesus was unimpressed with the tendency of his contemporaries to judge him, and he took this opportunity to remind them that, when we try to fit God's work into our models—when we judge God based on our own desires and expectations—we are likely to get things wrong. We are also, by way of human nature, impossible to please.

> "To what should I compare this generation? It's like children sitting in the marketplaces who call out to each other:

> We played the flute for you,
> but you didn't dance;
> we sang a lament,
> but you didn't mourn!
>
> For John did not come eating or drinking, and they say, 'He has a demon!' The Son of Man came eating and drinking, and they say, 'Look, a glutton and a drunkard, a friend of tax collectors and sinners!' Yet wisdom is vindicated by her deeds."[19]

A textual variant renders that last verse, *Wisdom is vindicated by her children.* In other words, it is the final results of a thing that prove it right or not. It's much the same as something else Jesus said: *You will know the tree by its fruit.*[20] Or, to use an old English idiom, *The proof is in the pudding.* What God is doing might look bad or foolish in the moment. What his handful of chosen people are doing might look entirely wrongheaded and doomed to fail. But wait and see, Jesus is saying. To be clear, he wasn't asking for a reasonless faith—there were plenty of good reasons to think God was working through John and through Jesus. He was simply asking the people to wait and see how it all shook out. If the wisdom of God was at play here, the end of the story would make it clear.

There's a caution in this to those of us who would judge the work of God in our own day and in our own lives. To some extent, we are always in the middle of the story. If you've ever watched a movie or read a novel (and I'm assuming you have), you're familiar with that

---
19 Matthew 11:16–18
20 Matthew 7:16

middle bit where absolutely everything is going wrong and there is no possible way the good guys will win (or get married, or live happily ever after). Except they will, of course; we know that because we've seen so many stories, and the pattern is always the same. It always gets darkest before the dawn. In terms of story structure there's even a name for this: it's called the "bleakest moment" or "the darkest hour." Interestingly, it's also—often—the moment when the hero makes a pivotal decision that ultimately determines how the story will end. And nine times out of ten, that decision is just this—*The hero decides not to give up.*

When we are dealing with fear and doubt, even a crisis of faith, in our own lives, it is perhaps wise to stop and ask where we are. John the Baptist sent his question to Jesus in the midst of his own bleakest moment, and the ending of his life would depend on how he responded to Jesus's answer. His choice, unfortunately, wasn't "live or die; get out of prison or stay in"; that decision would be made for him. His choice was "stay in faith or get out." Remain in Jesus, or walk away. *Judge the story based on the darkest hour, or believe that wisdom will justify her children—and be willing to change your understanding of the story itself if you need to.*

The darkest hour always looks like an ending. But Jesus challenges us to believe it isn't, that it's just a turning point along the way. Remember, the context of this entire conversation is Jesus calling people to take up their crosses and come, follow him—to *die*. And yet Jesus implies that if they do, death won't be the end of the story. As far as they understood it, death on a cross was absolutely, unequivocally the wrong ending for a story about the Messiah. It was so wrong that if the Messiah died, he couldn't have been the Messiah after all. But Jesus is basically saying, *Don't let appearances deceive you. You had good reasons to begin this journey of faith. See it out to the end.*

Because the end just might surprise you.

THE ARM OF THE LORD REVEALED

Earlier, we looked at one of the passages where Yahweh declared his intention to come and redeem his people, personally triumphing over their enemies. The passage was Isaiah 59:15-16 and following:

> The Lord saw that there was no justice,
> and He was offended.
> He saw that there was no man—
> He was amazed that there was no one interceding;
> so His own arm brought salvation,
> and His own righteousness supported Him.

Interestingly, this isn't the only time "the arm of the Lord" appears in Isaiah. Although the word "arm" in Scripture usually suggests strength and action, in Isaiah's writings it too takes on the idea of something hidden that will be revealed. First in Isaiah 52:10:

> The Lord has displayed His holy arm
> in the sight of all the nations;
> all the ends of the earth will see
> the salvation of our God.

But then—stunningly—*in Isaiah 53*. The fourth Servant Song, with its awful picture of suffering, rejection, and death, is also the place where the arm of the Lord is revealed.

> Who has believed what we have heard?
> And who has the arm of the Lord been revealed to?
> He grew up before Him like a young plant
> and like a root out of dry ground.
> He didn't have an impressive form
> or majesty that we should look at Him,
> no appearance that we should desire Him.
> He was despised and rejected by men,
> a man of suffering who knew what sickness was.
> He was like someone people turned away from;
> He was despised, and we didn't value Him.[21]

Reading this, I can't help but see a striking contrast to the "Little Horn" of Daniel's vision. In the symbolism of the Old Testament, both an "arm" and a "horn" represent strength and power. One is a specifically human picture, while the other is animalistic. In Daniel's "Little Horn," we have an animalistic power with the implication of "little strength"—yet the horn successfully oppresses the people of God through the power of its mouth. By speaking loud, arrogant, and blasphemous words, it makes war with the saints and prevails over them for a long time. In sharp contrast, the "arm of the Lord" is human and hidden. He does not call attention to himself. Remember the beginning of the first Servant Song:

> This is My Servant; I strengthen Him,
> this is My Chosen One; I delight in Him.
> I have put My Spirit on Him;
> He will bring justice to the nations.

---

[21] Isaiah 53:1–3

> He will not cry out or shout
> or make His voice heard in the streets.
> He will not break a bruised reed,
> and He will not put out a smoldering wick;
> He will faithfully bring justice.
> He will not grow weak or be discouraged
> until He has established justice on earth.
> The islands will wait for His instruction.[22]

When John the Baptist sent his message to Jesus, the arm of the Lord was still, to a great degree, hidden. Jesus simply didn't trumpet his identity or his intentions—unlike the enemy, whose accusations, slander, and threats were (and are) long and loud. So to see the wisdom of God at work, one would have to lean in close. Listen. Watch. Ponder. And wait.

The answer Jesus sent back to John the Baptist was not a loud, colorful, boastful one. It was the kind of answer that required pondering. The words of Jesus still do; the work of God still does. And even now, this is frequently the nexus of doubt: we want an answer, a clear one, now. We want the story to go the way we expected it to go. And instead we are presented with an invitation to lean in close, to reconsider our position, to understand something we have never understood before.

At times, that act of reconsideration might itself feel like a crisis. After all, if we reconsider the story, we might need to question pieces we have always taken as bedrock before.

But that isn't necessarily a bad thing. Doubt can feel immensely threatening. And it can *be* immensely threat-

---

[22] Isaiah 42:1–4

ening, especially if it becomes a capitulation to the long, loud, threatening, and arrogant words of the "Little Horn"—the Herods and Jezebels and Roman emperors and secular philosophies in our own lives.

But doubt can also pose an invitation. It can be an opportunity to renew our faith, and perhaps to renew it on stronger grounds. Doubt, in other words, can act as a purging, leaving us with a stronger and purer faith. If nothing else, it can reveal to us that our understanding is fallible. That's why, ultimately, it's not *what* we believe that matters so much as *who* we believe. "Faith in Christ" is not a creedal statement or a set of intellectual agreements. It's trust in a person. When John asked, "Are you the One?", Jesus's answer amounted to, "Yes, but trust *me*. This isn't going to go down the way you think."

THE REFINER'S FIRE

Sometime before Matthew 11, when Jesus's ministry was just beginning, the crowds of people who were drawn to John the Baptist wondered if *he* was the Messiah. Rumor had it that he might be, and they wanted to know—was he the one, or should they look for another? So John answered them:

> I baptize you with water, but One is coming who is more powerful than I. I am not worthy to untie the strap of His sandals. He will baptize you with the Holy Spirit and fire. His winnowing shovel is in His hand to clear His threshing floor and gather the wheat into His barn, but the chaff He will burn up

with a fire that never goes out.[23]

In his lecture "The Holy Spirit in Luke and Acts," Dr. Darrell Bock explains the image of "fire":

> The idea of fire is the picture of purging, the purging of humanity. Some get through the purging and survive it, and others are judged as a result of it. So there's this division of humanity that comes, and the dividing line is the gift of the Spirit that comes to those who respond to Jesus in faith.[24]

When the Messiah came, he would have the effect of separating wheat from chaff, silver from dross, belief from unbelief, believer from unbeliever, the righteous from the unrighteous. The purging would go through all levels of human experience, from the highest levels of society to the greatest depths of the individual human heart. But John wasn't the first to connect the Messiah's coming with a purging or refining by fire. That was the prophet Malachi, some four hundred years before—in a passage we've already looked at.

Before we get there, though, let's look again at Jesus's response to John's question in Matthew 11. After he sent back Isaiah 61 to John, Jesus turned to the crowds and said:

> What did you go out into the wilderness to see? A reed swaying in the wind? What then did you go out to see? A man dressed in soft clothes? Look, those who wear soft clothes are in kings' palaces. But what did you go out to see? A prophet? Yes, I

---

[23] Luke 3:16–17
[24] Dr. Darrell Bock, "The Holy Spirit in Luke and Acts," as heard on the *Master Lectures Podcast* by Zondervan Academic, December 3, 2019.

tell you, and far more than a prophet. This is the one it is written about:

Look, I am sending My messenger ahead of You;
he will prepare Your way before You.[25]

Before writing this book, I had read that passage a million times and never looked up the rest of the quote—the passage that Jesus spoke out in this scene. Actually, I just assumed the reference was to Isaiah 40. But it isn't. Jesus was quoting Malachi 3.

And look again at the rest of the passage:

"See, I am going to send My messenger, and he will clear the way before Me. Then the Lord you seek will suddenly come to His temple, the Messenger of the covenant you desire—see, He is coming," says the Lord of Hosts. But who can endure the day of His coming? And who will be able to stand when He appears? For He will be like a refiner's fire and like cleansing lye. He will be like a refiner and purifier of silver; He will purify the sons of Levi and refine them like gold and silver. Then they will present offerings to the Lord in righteousness. And the offerings of Judah and Jerusalem will please the Lord as in days of old and years gone by.[26]

When I first realized the connection between this prophetic passage and the narrative of Matthew 11, it took my breath away. Jesus was not only identifying John on the landscape of prophetic history, he was also explaining the interaction of this very moment. John, the messenger of Yahweh, had come to clear the way be-

---

25 Matthew 11:7–10
26 Malachi 3:1–4

fore the Messiah. The Messiah, the Lord, had come to his temple—just as the people sought. And in an unimaginable twist, the Messiah was not just a human king but Yahweh himself, setting up his kingdom on earth and bringing a new covenant era to his people. But even as Malachi prophesied, the coming of the Lord brought with it a refining fire—a trial and testing that would burn away impurities from his servants. And then, in a breathtaking moment of clarity, Jesus reveals that John the Baptist, the Forerunner and Messenger, would be the first to undergo the refining.

But who can endure the day of His coming? And who will be able to stand when He appears? For He will be like a refiner's fire and like cleansing lye. He will be like a refiner and purifier of silver; He will purify the sons of Levi and refine them like gold and silver. Remember, John the Baptist was a Levite—the son of a priest. For hundreds and thousands of years since the day they were called to serve Yahweh as his set-apart tribe within a set-apart people, the Levites had been sometimes faithful and oftentimes corrupt. But when the Messiah came, Malachi prophesied, he would begin the work of purifying with his most sanctified servants.

John the Baptist, the Levite. The forerunner of our doubts—and the forerunner of our refining.

The End of One Road

Not long after John's disciples brought Jesus's riddling answer from Isaiah 61 back to him in prison, John reached the end of his earthly road.

Centuries before, when Elijah complained to God that Jezebel was hunting him down to kill him, God essentially rebuked him for his unbelief. Elijah fled into the wilderness, profoundly encountered God, and lived at least seven more years before his time arrived to go up to God in heaven. He passed out of this world in peace and victory, carried into the heavens in a flaming chariot while his awestruck disciple, Elisha, watched.

It wasn't anything like that for John.

John had been thrown into prison because he confronted Herod over his immoral relationship with Herodias, Herod's sister-in-law. But Herod was afraid of John and even somewhat fascinated by him. He threw him in prison, but he didn't have the guts to kill him. Herodias was different. She was hateful and vindictive. She saw a chance to turn Herod's insecurities against him, and she baited him into ordering John's death at a feast in order to save face in front of his guests.

John was beheaded in prison, and his head was put on a platter and presented to Herodias at the party.

His doubts never got an answer in this world beyond the one Jesus sent him. The one that wasn't completely clear, but gave John reasons to hope and to renew his faith that God was truly acting through his cousin.

We don't know if that answer brought John peace. If it laid his fears and doubts to rest. We don't know for certain whether he came through the refiner's fire with a stronger faith—though I believe that he did.

We do know that in future years, his disciples and

Jesus's disciples essentially merged. The followers of John the Baptist became "Christians," a word derived from *Christ*, the Greek word for "Messiah." Eventually, after Jesus was raised from the dead, they were all convinced it was true. John had been right. Jesus was the Messiah. The new era had come.

But John didn't see it. Not from this side of the veil, anyway.

Your Doubts, in the Story of God

You started reading this book for a reason. It might be a purely academic one, but chances are good that it isn't. Chances are good you're reading this book because you are a follower of Jesus, or you have been one or you want to be one, but you are wrestling with doubt. You fear it may all be a lie. And even if it isn't, because you wrestle with doubt, because you experience crisis, because you don't have it all figured out, you are afraid you may be disqualified.

But in the story of God, the story of Jesus, your doubts are not unexpected. They are certainly not unprecedented. Jesus answered John's disciples and said, "Go and report to John what you hear and see: the blind see, the lame walk, those with skin diseases are healed, the deaf hear, the dead are raised, and the poor are told the good news. *And if anyone is not offended because of Me, he is blessed.*"[27] When Jesus comes, he baptizes with the Holy Spirit and with fire. Doubt—offense—crisis—the moment when the story goes sideways and you are

---
27 Matthew 11:4–6

no longer sure you are standing on solid ground. *This is the refiner's fire.*

Can we shortcut this fire or avoid going through it? I don't know. Maybe. Maybe not every believer walks the same road. *(Certainly* not every believer walks the same road.) The author of Hebrews wrote:

At that time his voice shook the earth, but now he has promised, "Yet once more I will shake not only the earth but also the heavens." This phrase, "Yet once more," indicates the removal of things that are shaken—that is, things that have been made—in order that the things that cannot be shaken may remain. Therefore let us be grateful for receiving a kingdom that cannot be shaken, and thus let us offer to God acceptable worship, with reverence and awe, for our God is a consuming fire.[28]

If the very heavens and earth will be shaken, then surely we need to know that we will be too. Just as John the Baptist, the son of Levi, was called upon to surrender his story—his understanding of the work and will of God—to a greater story, to the hidden work and will of God that were more than he could ever have imagined, so we too are called to release the stories we cling to and let them be purified in the refiner's fire. We may find ourselves called upon to relinquish beliefs and expectations that have seemed critical for us, to trust in *who* more than we trust in *what.*

Also implied by this is the reality that God and his kingdom are capable of withstanding the fire. If we are willing to surrender and if we resist becoming of-

---

28 Hebrews 12:26–19

fended and standing on our offense, the end of the crisis will not be the loss of everything. We will lose only that which can be shaken, that which is dross and can be burned away. What remains will be silver and gold. What remains will be a kingdom that cannot be shaken.

Daniel saw the kingdom of God given to the holy ones of the Most High. He saw it grow and become a great mountain and fill the whole earth. If we are to have a faith that remains, if our feet are truly to stand on level ground, then we can't escape the fire. We can't simply choose never to struggle, to doubt, or to fear that we are wrong. We can't spend a lifetime stuffing down our doubts and never letting our beliefs be purified. We have to go *through* the refiner's fire.

No matter how terrifying it may, in the moment, seem.

At the end of Matthew 11 are a prayer and a promise.

> At that time Jesus declared, "I thank you, Father, Lord of heaven and earth, that you have hidden these things from the wise and understanding and revealed them to little children; yes, Father, for such was your gracious will. All things have been handed over to me by my Father, and no one knows the Son except the Father, and no one knows the Father except the Son and anyone to whom the Son chooses to reveal him. Come to me, all who labor and are heavy laden, and I will give you rest. Take my yoke upon you, and learn from me, for I am gentle and lowly in heart, and you will find rest for your souls. For my yoke is easy, and my burden is light."[29]

---

29 Matthew 11:25–30, ESV

At the end of the fire is purity. At the end of our story, once we have relinquished it, is the self-revelation of God—the unveiling of the mystery prepared for us, the hidden future that no eye had seen nor ear heard until Jesus himself lived it out. At the end of the struggle is rest.

But the way cannot be avoided. It can't be dodged or ducked or climbed over. The only way through the fire is *through*.

Chapter 9:
The Way Through: Choosing Faith Over Doubt When There Are Reasons for Both

I hope by now it is clear that I am not advocating we do all we can to avoid our doubts and stuff them down. I am fairly certain that every believer struggles with doubt, sometimes very *serious* doubt, and stuffing it only leads to long-term cracks in our foundation—to a deep and built-in weakness in the very places we need to be strong.

I am instead advocating that we face our doubts, name them and bring them into the light. It is good to wrestle with what we believe. That's how we discover things we've missed. It's how we go deeper and learn more. It's how we come to trade our old stories for God's new one. If we have specific questions, we should seek out answers. We should pray, and read, and ask others for their perspectives, and humble ourselves enough to grow.

But when we do all this, we should know that eventually we'll have a choice to make. A friend of mine, a Bible teacher named Alan Gilman, once told me, "I think it's time we stop doubting our beliefs and believing our doubts. We need to believe our beliefs and doubt our doubts." I don't know if he came up with that or heard it from someone else, but it's wise—immensely so. Eventually we'll need to stop the wrestle and embrace what we believe as wholeheartedly as we can. Here's the thing, though: this is not about simply pretending we don't doubt or attempting to shore up our beliefs with apologetics, fleeces, or communal encouragement (all of which have their place). It's about getting honest and then choosing to believe anyway, when we have seen that there are sufficient reasons to believe—and that there are also sufficient reasons to doubt.

John the Baptist's warning about the Messiah's fire and winnowing fork is frightening for a reason: *not everyone makes it through*. Some, faced with doubts, will *choose* their doubts. They will place their faith in them. They will believe their doubts, and they will be lost.

Others, faced with doubts, will choose Jesus.

Notice I didn't say they will choose their old story about Jesus. It would not have done John the Baptist any good to cling to his old paradigm about exactly what the Messiah would look like and do, no matter how literal and biblical and conservative that story was. That story came straight from Scripture, yes—but it was missing pieces and others were hiding, and so the version of it that John thought he knew was wrong. It was like trying to get the correct answer in a math equation when several of the factors are missing; it just won't work until all the pieces are in place. And so some, faced with doubts, will realize that they *do not* understand everything and they *cannot* understand everything because even though we see vast horizons further than John did, we are still in the middle of the story and not all of the pieces are in place yet.

No matter how many true things we know, and no matter how important those true things may be (truth is always important), ultimately our faith cannot be in our particular understanding of a message. It must be in the Man. It must be in Jesus, the One who was to come. So rather than believe their doubts, some will believe in Jesus and believe *that* belief—that he can be trusted, no matter how unclear the story looks from here.

THE SUMMONS TO SEEK

Over the years, many have asked why God does not just make the truth plain and obvious. Why doesn't he just appear in the sky in a big, explosive vision, declaring himself beyond any shadow of a doubt? I don't know the answer to that question, but I can say that it appears he does not do that because, on some grand scale having to do with his wisdom and character, that is just not how God operates. Jesus said:

> Don't give what is holy to dogs or toss your pearls before pigs, or they will trample them with their feet, turn, and tear you to pieces. Keep asking, and it will be given to you. Keep searching, and you will find. Keep knocking, and the door will be opened to you. For everyone who asks receives, and the one who searches finds, and to the one who knocks, the door will be opened.[1]

---

1 Matthew 7:6–8

There is something in the nature of God that honors holy things by reserving them for those who will likewise honor them—something that hides truth so that seekers will value it, invest their time and their efforts and their hearts in it, and find it. It's not an accident that truth ends up hidden or even that God himself ends up hidden; it's a part of his will. It's meant to draw us out, with our energies and or interest, the way a woman in an old-fashioned love story draws out a man's energies and interest by holding back, revealing herself only little by little as he pursues her. Finally, she will reveal herself fully and give herself fully only when he commits himself, entirely, to her. It is much the same way in our dance with the divine. The hiddenness of truth is a summons to seek.

If we accept the scriptural account as true, there was one moment in history when God essentially *did* show up and say, "Here I am; you can't ignore me"—and that was Jesus's resurrection. But fascinatingly, on the same day Jesus rose from the dead, an alternative "truth" was also released into the world. In Matthew 28:9–10, we read of Jesus's explosive encounter with the women at his tomb, including a promise to meet with the rest of his disciples. But immediately after that, Matthew records that the guards who had been watching over the tomb where Jesus lay went into the city with a message of their own:

> While the women were on their way, some of the guards went into the city and reported to the chief priests everything that had happened. When the chief priests had met with the elders and devised

a plan, they gave the soldiers a large sum of money, telling them, "You are to say, 'His disciples came during the night and stole him away while we were asleep.' If this report gets to the governor, we will satisfy him and keep you out of trouble." So the soldiers took the money and did as they were instructed. And this story has been widely circulated among the Jews to this very day.[2]

The fact of Jesus's resurrection was *immediately* countered with an alternative "truth." From that day forward, anyone who heard the story of his resurrection would be offered a counter-story, one that on the face of it seemed far more reasonable. "Haven't you heard? That was just a story invented by his followers so they wouldn't be discredited. What *actually* happened was that his disciples stole his body away during the night. You can ask the soldiers yourself—they're around here somewhere."

Interestingly, this idea of truth and counter-truth was evident early in Jesus's life and ministry as well, when the Pharisees found it easy to dismiss him on the basis of his birthplace. "Search and look," they said; "no prophet comes from Galilee."[3] They were looking for a Messiah from Bethlehem in Judea, the City of David, as prophesied by Micah 5:2. But it would not have taken *much* digging for them to realize that while he was raised in Nazareth, a city in Galilee without any apparent prophetic significance, Jesus had in fact been born in Bethlehem. A simple question to one of his neighbors

---

[2] Matthew 28:11–15
[3] John 7:52

or relatives would have told them that. But rather than ask, they took the more convenient answer and left the truth uncovered.

It seems to me that this idea of story and counter-story, truth and its alternative, runs throughout the history of the world and is in fact a spiritual principle of sorts. Why? Perhaps to preserve the role of choice in our relationship with God. We always have to choose, and any true choice requires more than one option.

None of this is to say, of course, that some things aren't actually *true,* and that other things aren't actually *false.* The choices are not equally valid, and truth *can* be found. But it takes seeking to figure it out. *(Ask, seek, knock.)* In the story of the tomb, the truth was there for the looking, but only those who cared enough to put in the effort would ever find it. Everyone else would simply settle for the easier answer—the alternative offered to them.

Moreover, even though truth can be found, not all truth is of the scientifically quantifiable, measurable-with-the-mind-and-the-right-instruments kind. Some truth has to be discovered with the heart; some truth has to be trusted in order to be fully known. This is the kind of truth that is relational—the kind that is expressed in the words "I love you" or "I'm on your side." It can't be boiled down to formulae. Its language is that of self-revelation and of informed decisions to trust.

John's question, "Are you the One who is to come?", set up an interesting dilemma. Jesus had not openly declared himself to be the Messiah, but he had been saying and doing many things that strongly pointed to that conclusion. He had been openly and publicly working miracles, demonstrating supernatural power over nature, disease, and demons. He had demonstrated a profound understanding of the Scriptures and taught with unusual authority. On top of that, John had personal reasons to believe—things God had supernaturally revealed to him, not to mention his own miraculous conception, the angelic visits surrounding his birth and that of Jesus, and the prophecies his father Zechariah had given. So we have to wonder: What could Jesus have said or done that would have satisfied John? What exactly would have put his doubts to rest?

On the same level, what could God do that would satisfy *us*?

When we are wrestling with doubt, we tend to want one of two things (or, ideally, both). First, we want some kind of quantifiable proof. Second, we want a personal answer that explains things well enough, and reveals God's *heart* deeply enough, to give our hearts peace and rest in the midst of our pain and our struggle.

Often, we mistake one for the other. We think that proof of God's existence would satisfy our hearts, or that if we had a deep inner revelation of his love, it would lay to rest our more scientific questions. I don't think this is case. In fact, our hearts and our minds live in (healthy) tension with one another, and doubt exists in this tension. We need reason and rationality—but in a relational universe, our demands for proof can quickly become unreasonable. It's all too easy to be like the Pharisees of Jesus's day, who had witnessed his incredible miracles and power and yet still insisted that they needed a "sign" before they would believe in him. And we need revelation and personal experience, but they can't settle all our questions—in fact they may just raise more.

For us, living in the modern world, doubt comes in from avenues John did not have to deal with. No one in his day seriously questioned the existence of God (at least, not in Judea). Religious pluralism and changing morality were huge issues in the first-century Roman world, but at least most people took the existence of the spiritual world for granted. In our day, that's not so; and we are far enough from the first century that some even question the existence or nature of the *people* who lived in it—Jesus, especially. In the first century, there was no claim that "science" could explain everything (although philosophy made a good run at the job). The secular, atheistic bent of the modern West can raise serious questions for us, as can globalism and the return of a pluralistic society. But at the same time, we continue to wrestle with deeper questions, the same heart-level questions that have always mattered to human beings. We want to know if there is a God, not as a matter of scientific inquiry, but as the most pressing question of our souls. We want to know if there is a God because we need to know who *we* are, and if we are loved, and if we are wanted. Those are not questions we will ever answer with a calculator or a microscope.

There Are Reasons for Belief and Reasons for Doubt

The God of the Bible never asked anyone to engage in trust that had no basis. When John sent his question to Jesus, the answer Jesus sent back was not the equivalent of "reason has nothing to do with faith, so just shut your eyes and believe."

One characteristic of a Christian worldview—based as it is on historical events in the real, geographical world and on the written statements of Scripture about those events—is the belief that some things are actually true and other things are not; that truth exists and can be known, and that yes, this matters. Following on that, Christians also believe that truth can be grasped by human reason, and that in fact the universe in general is reasonable and understandable, because it was created by a reasonable and understandable God. (It was this Christian belief that historically gave birth to Western science, and yes, that's ironic.)

Jesus's answer to John follows the same pattern as Yahweh's self-revelation in the Old Testament when he appeared to Abraham, for example, or to Moses. In every case God demonstrated enough about himself and about his power and righteousness to give the human beings he was calling into relationship a rational basis for belief. It wasn't an *exhaustive* basis for belief—there was always some room for doubt. But it was enough. It set up the same kind of choice we make, and chance we take, when we choose to trust that another human being will keep their word or come through for us, based on what we know about their character and abilities. We make a decision, based not on *nothing,* but not based on absolute certainty either. We make a decision, based on something-that-is-enough, that we will trust. Then we can only wait to see whether our trust has been justified or not.

So Jesus did not ask John to believe without reason. Instead, he pointed out miraculous actions he was actually doing in the real world, and he showed how they were connected to prophecy in the Scripture. He was doing things John's disciples could bear witness to and tell John about. His answer would also have reminded John of the things he had personally seen and heard: the dove, the voice from heaven. Jesus gave John real reasons to believe, even though he didn't explain away all the reasons for doubt.

And this is the paradox we all live in. When it comes to truth, of the transcendent and eternal kind, there are reasons to believe—real reasons, good reasons. There are things we can know. Logic, wisdom, and intellect all have a place in faith. And yet, there are also reasons to doubt. God does not take away every possibility that we could be wrong, that our faith could be misguided. Instead he asks for trust. Again, this is not unfair, even though it may sound that way at first blush. It's commensurate with the kind of God we have, the kind of creatures we are, and the kind of thing faith is. Faith, at its core, is relational. It is not an intellectual exercise (as though the human intellect could ever fully grasp and dissect the transcendent and eternal). Faith is the currency of giving and receiving, of demonstrated character and of reciprocal trust. Faith, as Paul put it in Galatians 5:6, works by love.

So yes—there are many reasons to believe in God, and many reasons to believe the God of Christianity is *the* God, the real and true one. Some of these reasons are good; some less so. But this is not a book of apologetics, and I can't make an exhaustive survey of all these reasons here. Suffice it to say: nearly every question anyone has ever asked about the existence of God or about the great philosophical questions of, say, miracles or suffering or life-after-death has been answered. Seek and you will find. (The answers are not even particularly difficult to get hold of; you can judge for yourself how good they are or aren't.) When it comes to trusting Jesus, or choosing belief over doubt, I'm not talking about shutting our eyes to reality and singing "la-la-la, I can't hear you" until the things that are troubling us go away. In my opinion, Christians get into a lot of trouble by doing exactly that. Reason does have a role; evidence does play a role. And as I've said—there is plenty of evidence pointing toward theism generally and Christianity specifically as *true*.

But I think we need to realize that where something appears to be true, an alternative will always suggest itself as also possible; and by the very design of the universe, we will never be able to lay all our doubts to rest through "proof." I'm not sure we *can* prove God. If God showed up for us in a huge display of power and glory, how could we prove that we weren't hallucinating? If he healed us, how could we absolutely prove our healing didn't have some other hidden cause?

Evidence is valuable, but evidence cannot be evenly deployed. We can prove the efficacy of medicine or the existence of an insect or an atom or a star, but we can't prove the existence of love—and we deal with love every day, in ways that are hugely consequential to us. We regularly pin all our hopes, dreams, and fears on love, and we can't quantify love at all or even really explain it. I can't prove that I love you; I can only demonstrate that I do. You can't prove it either; you can only trust in what I say and do, or more fundamentally, you can only trust in what you know of *me*. Risk can never be completely removed. And yet love, like wisdom, is justified by its effects.

In the nature of our universe, nothing that really matters to us is provable in an absolute sense. I can't even prove beyond a shadow of a doubt that I exist, or that you do. I believe those things, and I have good reasons to believe them; but I can't *prove* them. That's the way life is here. Once we have laid down a basic foundation of evidence and reasonable probability, everything else is based on trust. This isn't just true of God or "religion" but even of human relationships. Everything that matters is a matter of faith.

But in *fact*, most of our doubts are of a far more personal kind. They are not just intellectual exercises; they are personal crises of faith—of trust in a person called God. And for these, the answers are relational, just as the crisis is relational. In a sense, we don't doubt what God has done so much as we doubt what he has meant by it.

And if we're truly honest, most of our doubts aren't really about the logical, philosophical, or scientific questions that occur to us (or even sometimes plague us). For those doubts that truly are rooted in those areas, real answers do exist—if we faithfully seek them out, we will find them. And it's not about trying to make facts fit our worldview. There are honest answers to honest questions. After all, if there *is* no rational basis for Christianity, then we are crazy to entertain the whole thing and we really should stop it and get honest about reality. If on the other hand we are committed to seeking out *truth*, honest answers are nonnegotiable.

THE MEANING OF IT ALL

Behind every argument over facts or science or philosophy or comparative religion is another, deeper question. Take creation, for example. We can know, about as surely as we can know anything, that there is a creator, simply by virtue of the fact that there is a creation. At times science has tried to say that the universe has emerged from nothing, but that is manifestly absurd. All arguments about Genesis 1 and literalism and time frames and processes aside—everything about the known, physical universe tells us that it can't have created itself, nor is time sufficient to have done the job without any materials or forces at play to begin with. (There's an old story about a scientist who tells God that he's not so hot; after all, man can create life in a test tube now. So God says that he and the man will have a competition: they will each create a living being. God and the man kneel down and start to gather up dirt to form into a body, but God stops the man and said, "Hey, get your own dirt.")

Twenty-three hundred years ago, Aristotle recognized this basic philosophical idea. He referred to the beginner of the universe as the "Unmoved Mover" or the "First Cause." St. Thomas Aquinas, in his thirteenth-century treatise *Summa Theologica*, formulated the concept like this:

> In the world, we can see that things are caused. But it is not possible for something to be the cause of itself because this would entail that it exists prior to itself, which is a contradiction. If that by which it is caused is *itself* caused, then it too must have a cause. But this cannot be an infinitely long chain, so, there must be a cause which is not itself caused by anything further. This everyone understands to be God.[4]

In his book *Knowing Christ Today: Why We Can Trust Spiritual Knowledge*, Dallas Willard asks us to picture the universe as a line of dominos stretching as far as we can see in either direction. In one direction every domino has fallen; in the other they are still standing. In front of you, one domino is knocking the next one over. The theological (and scientific) question is, *What made the first domino fall?*

Fundamentally, there must be a god, with "god" very loosely defined as something outside of the universe that caused the universe. We know this because there is

---

[4] St. Thomas Aquinas, "Argument of the First Cause," *Summa Theologica*. As quoted in Frederick Copleston, S.J., *A History of Philosophy, Vol. 2: Medieval Philosophy—From Augustine to Duns Scotus* (New York: Image, 1993), 341–342.

a universe. *We are here.* To use Willard's image, the dominos *are* falling. There is a you and there is a me; there is a sky and an earth and stars and physical laws and forces and life. It is nonsense to say nothing knocked the first domino down, that there was nothing there and nothing happened. It can't simply be an infinite line with no beginning, because if it were, no domino would fall. The fact that something is happening now, something is *here* now, means something began to happen in the past. This universe as we know it is not capable of producing itself. Therefore "God," whoever or whatever "God" is, does exist and has acted in history to produce the universe in which we live.

We don't know, on this basis alone, anything much about what this God is like. We don't necessarily know if he is a "he" or an "it" or anything like that. We don't know how "he" created or why, or if questions like how and why or words like "created" even apply to the kind of thing this First Cause is. I think it's reasonable to believe that a God capable of causing a complex creation like this one is highly intelligent and intentional as well as powerful and transcendent (i.e., existing outside of this universe), but you might argue that he (or it) is simply powerful and transcendent—some kind of strong causative force outside of the known universe and not governed by its laws, but also without intentionality or personality or will. Many have argued as much.

It's true that science can't see God. It can't measure him or detect him. But this proves nothing about the existence of God one way or the other, because science is an approach for measuring and describing the physical world, and if God exists, he must by nature be outside of the physical world. I can't see in the dark; that doesn't mean the world ceases to exist when the lights go out. It just means my eyes aren't constructed to see without light. In the same way, science is not capable of "seeing" anything outside of the physical world. Science is an approach to the physical world that allows us to quantify, measure, and describe objects within the physical universe. Anything that is outside of the physical universe is, by nature, not visible to science and not measurable by scientific means.

And interestingly, even before there was such a thing as science as we know it now, the Bible insisted that God was outside of the physical universe—that he was "holy," set apart, entirely Other. "I Am That I Am," God says when asked his name.[5] The Bible (unlike some other major religions) has always insisted that the God who created the universe is also unlike the universe; he is not made of stuff that science can *see*. And rather obviously, if science can't see God, then it shouldn't be any surprise when scientists say they don't see him. We should in fact expect that. So although it's a commonly held idea these days that science has somehow disproven God, if we're honest we have to confess that's impossible. Science *cannot* disprove the existence of God. If God exists, he is outside of science's field of vision.

But let's say we accept all of that as true. Let's say we embrace the idea that God is real, and that we can know that based on the existence of the universe. That does not answer all our questions—far from it. It may

---

5 Exodus 3:14

even raise more. Many people today, even in the West, have fully accepted the idea that a god or gods must exist. They have grasped this idea that the realm of spirit is real—so we have the New Age movement, or the vague idea that all religions lead to the same place, or the popular notion of being spiritual but not religious. Many people speak of the universe as though it *is* God—as though it is somehow guiding or helping or defining them. In my opinion, all this points to the inability of science to tell us what we really want, and need, to know.

In a very real sense, the idea of God as creator doesn't *mean* anything to us, it says nothing to assuage our real doubts and answer our real questions, until a relational dimension enters the picture. It doesn't mean anything until the day we hear a voice in creation calling our names. It may even make us angry to know that someone or something created us, if, for example, we reject ourselves or feel bitter about our lives. It doesn't mean anything to be told that God has created us until we learn to see creation, and even ourselves, our own inner being and makeup, as a gift to us from someone who cares. The songwriter Andrew Peterson asks, "Don't you want to thank someone?"[6] We aren't lost, and angry, and feeling the frustrations of John in prison because we're not sure whether maple trees sprang from intention or by accident. We're feeling all these things because we're not sure whether the will behind the universe is good; because we don't know if he sees us; because we're not sure if we want him to.

---

6 Andrew Peterson, "Don't You Want to Thank Someone?" From the album *Light for the Lost Boy*, 2012.

If science cannot see God because God is outside of and "other than" the universe and therefore is not detectable by physical means, we might rightly wonder if that means we are cut off from knowledge of God. After all, we are physical beings with physical senses. We are made of scientific stuff. But that isn't *all* we're made of. We do in fact operate, every day, in a realm that science can't see or measure. We are tangible and physical, but we are also intangible and spiritual. For human beings, most of life is lived on the inside.[7] We imagine. We make. We intend. We think. We will. We choose. We act. We know, and we are known. We love, and we are loved. We are something of an anomaly in the world. We are a puzzle that science is still trying hard to understand. And we are equipped to know God, to hear him, to love him, and to trust. Or at least, that is what the Bible claims.

FROM CREATION TO CROSS

Years ago Francis Schaeffer wrote a book and called it *The God Who Is There*. It was an argument against many modern philosophies and worldviews that claim God is absent or cut off from us. Taking the argument further, he wrote a second book called *He Is There, and He Is Not Silent*. The idea is this: It would be perfectly reasonable to assume that "God" who caused this universe simply stepped away from it and decided to stay uninvolved.

---

[7] As singer/songwriter Misty Edwards has pointed out in much of her work, including her book *What Is the Point?: Discovering Life's Deeper Meaning and Purpose* (Lake Mary, FL: Charisma House, 2013) and the 2014 song "Audience of One."

It would be just as reasonable to assume he is not a being we could ever possibly access or understand anyway. Reasonable—but lots of things are reasonable that turn out not to be true. It would be perfectly reasonable to assume that I don't write—I don't have to, do I? But as it turns out, I do write. A reasonable thesis that I do not write falls apart as soon as someone provides you with evidence that I do.

And this is what the stories in the Bible are: they are evidence. They are a claim, from history, that God is not uninvolved, and he is not unknowable. He has not stayed at a distance. He is there, and he is not silent. The stories of the Bible (and the many, many, many stories of Christians since then) claim that God can be known, heard, seen, and related to by human beings. They claim in fact that God wants relationship; that he has, at various points in history, formed formal relationships called covenants with human beings and with nations and that he has given people many reasons to believe in him and to trust his word and his nature. They also claim that the God of the Bible, revealed in Jesus Christ, is *the* God, and that he has revealed his nature in such a way that most of the claims of the "spiritual but not believing" crowd are seen to be bankrupt.

And here our own journeys crop back up, maybe carrying with them anger or fear or abandonment—*But he hasn't given me reasons. But I don't trust him, and he doesn't keep his word. And I don't know how to deal with what I am feeling because of it.*

Those are big feelings. Let's sit with them for a moment. Allow them to be here. Bring them along on the journey, and not cut them off or try to answer them prematurely. Let's just keep going with this conversation.

So according to the claims of Christianity, God has shown up in history, and his actions and words have been recorded by people, and that is what the Bible is. Some other religions also make claims about God doing things in history, although usually not in a way that is much at all like the claims of the Bible in terms of historicity and geography and that kind of thing—in other words, what most religions say about the actions of God or gods are more like fables, intended to teach something but not really located in this world or in history as we know it. The closest I can think to a historical claim is the claim of Islam that Allah gave the Quran to Mohammed through an angel, on a mountain outside of Mecca in Saudi Arabia, from about 609 to 632 AD. Real place, real time. Claims like this are qualitatively different from the claims of the world's other major religions: Hinduism, which is a decentralized and founderless collection of traditional practices and rituals, philosophies, and spiritual beliefs; or Buddhism, which is based on the philosophical teachings of a man who said he had achieved a profound inner experience of enlightenment. Most (not all) of the miracle claims, and the personal-encounter-with-a-personal-God claims, and the life-transformation claims, come from Christianity—and there is good reason for that. It points to what's unique about Christianity as a whole.

As we saw extensively in the first half of this book, in the long history of Israel before John the Baptist,

God promised over and over to act in a climactic, world-changing way in history. He promised what N.T. Wright calls "the Return of Yahweh." He promised to redeem his people, forgive their sins, and set them free; and he promised to bless the nations, to bring peace to the world, and to rule over all peoples on the face of the earth through his Anointed One.

Then silence, more than four hundred years of it.

Then John.

Then Jesus.

Then John was killed.

And then so was Jesus.

Here we have to pause. Some academics have tried to argue that Jesus was not a historical person, or that he didn't die on a cross. Most of those arguments have, by now, been long abandoned. The life of Jesus is incredibly well attested, and that he was executed by the Romans and died on a cross can be taken as fact without any particular faith required.[8]

But those are just facts. We can prove them, and they may not mean much to us. Why does it matter if a Jewish man, even a particularly wise, kind, and inspiring Jewish man, was killed on a cross two thousand years ago? The more important claim is the next one—three days after the death of Jesus, Christians by the dozens began to claim that he had been spontane-

---

8 Again, the information isn't hard to find. A few old standbys that serve as good places to start include Josh McDowell's *Evidence that Demands a Verdict* and Lee Strobel's *The Case for Christ*. For something a little more academic, I'm fond of *Can We Still Believe the Bible?* by Craig L. Blomberg.

ously resurrected. That he was alive, fully human, fully back in the flesh, and walking around in their midst, while also displaying capabilities that were more than human—walking through walls, appearing and disappearing, knowing the secret thoughts of people's hearts. Believe it or not, *this can also be proven to the same degree that any other fact of ancient history can be proven.*[9] Not only that, but *the dominos are still falling.* Something started the phenomenon we call Christianity. The earliest witnesses say that something was the resurrection of Jesus. No other explanation has ever come forward as sufficiently convincing.

THE ROAD FROM RESURRECTION

The fact of creation raises the issue of whether God is someone we can know—someone with a personality, a will, and an existence independent from ours—or just an impersonal force of some kind. The Bible, with its stories of the Creator God interacting with human beings, answers that question with a *yes,* he is knowable and *yes,* he has revealed himself to us. But the resurrection is where it all comes together. Nothing else in history has ever occurred that was like it, and it gives meaning to all that came before it and to all that comes after it.

The resurrection is what John the Baptist wanted to see but didn't. It is the demonstration that Jesus was who he said he was and that the crucifixion was something far more than it appeared to be on the surface.

---

9 Lee Strobel, *The Case for Christ: A Journalist's Personal Investigation of the Evidence for Jesus* (Grand Rapids: Zondervan, 2008; updated and expanded 2016).

And this means everything to us. It means everything to our questions, our doubts.

Wrestling in the Dark

I was a strange child, given to deep thoughts and existential insomnia. I remember one night on my grandparents' farm when I was trying to sleep, but my mind had been gripped with a question so disturbing I couldn't damp it down or move past it. I think I was about eight years old. I got up and went to sit on the side of the bathtub in the bathroom, because it helps to turn lights on when you're wrestling through an existential crisis, and I couldn't turn the lights on in my room because my sisters were asleep. And besides, if the adults saw the lights on in there late at night I would probably get in trouble.

My question was this: If God knew that Adam was going to sin, and he created him anyway, didn't that mean God had created sin?

This disturbed me deeply because somehow, even at that age and despite being raised in a loving and protected home, I knew that sin was dark and devastating and that it hurt people. If God had created sin, it seemed to make him responsible for all of that. And if God is responsible for darkness and devastation and hurting people, how can we possibly trust him?

I wanted to trust God. I wanted to know him and follow him. But in that hour sitting on the side of the bathtub in the middle of the night in rural Ontario, I just didn't know if I could.

To skip to the point, I didn't manage to figure out the question of God and sin and Adam. But I did wrestle back to the point of trust, and now, looking back, I'm sure it was the Holy Spirit who spoke to me and got me through. Here's what I saw that night:

I don't know the answer to this question, but I do know that if God's answer to sin was to become a man and suffer through all of our pain with us, then he can be trusted. Anyone who would respond to sin by seeking us out and allowing sin to hurt him too is someone whose heart I can trust.

I figured I would understand the rest someday. (I still hope that I will.) But I've never moved past that answer. I don't know how it all works. I don't know why God made the choices he did. But if God really did take on human flesh, if he really did make himself vulnerable and cold and poor, if he really did allow himself to be rejected and constantly misunderstood and slandered, if he really did volunteer to be stripped and beaten and crucified—and if he really did do all of this in order to suffer with us and love us and ultimately rescue us—then I can trust him.

Someone whose heart looks like Jesus has demonstrated love enough for me to trust him, even if I don't have every other piece of the puzzle yet.

The resurrection is important, of course, for many other reasons that I don't fully understand either. (There is a lot I don't fully understand.) But one of the reasons it's *most* important is what it says about Jesus's heart and all the things he did *before* the resurrection.

If the resurrection really happened, as every bit of historical evidence insists it did, it vindicates everything Jesus said about himself. It means God really was with him. It means his teachings and his claims really were true. And it means his death really meant what he said it meant.

Religious teachers can make a lot of claims. They can do a lot of good works, they can be convincing and persuasive and inspiring, they can sometimes do things we can't explain, and unfortunately, they can fake a lot if they are that kind of leader. *But they can't raise themselves from the dead.* If Jesus truly did come back from the grave, alive, healthy, healed, and full of the Holy Spirit, then we can and we *must* take everything he said seriously.

Perhaps most of all, we must take the cross seriously. In a very real sense, the answers are all in the cross. Just as the resurrection answers our philosophical and scientific questions through its occurrence in real history, so it is the cross that gives answers to our personal, relational, and theological questions. The cross was the answer for John the Baptist. It was the missing piece that made sense of all the prophecy and caused everything to fit, in a way that was completely unexpected and ran counter to all the best theories of biblical scholars. And in the same way, as we look back on the cross, we can see—if not the answers to our questions, at least the promise that the answer exists and that in time, it too will come.

The cross means we can trust Jesus, that if we suffer,

he is in our sufferings. It means that he meets us in our weakness and brokenness and yes, even in our doubts. It is here, in the darkness, that he defeats the darkness. In the cross, Jesus fulfilled and expanded every promise made to the human race—subversively and counterintuitively, he defeated death, forgave sin, and redeemed the captives through the freely given sacrifice of himself. Many have said that Jesus died to appease the Father somehow, as though the Father was vindictive and angry and had to be satisfied by blood. That view sees Jesus as offering himself as a sacrifice to the Father—and there is *some* truth to that. But even more, Jesus offered himself *to us*. In the ancient Hebrew sacrificial system, the people who bought the sacrifices also ate of those sacrifices. The sacrifices expressed worship to God but also fed and sanctified the people and brought them into fellowship with God. So it is with Jesus. He entered our pain and hunger and gave himself freely to meet our needs, not because of anger or vindication but because "God so loved the world."[10] *This is my body, broken for you,* Jesus said. *Take, eat.*[11]

Seeing the Story from the Other Side

We've spent a lot of time in this book unpacking the expectations of John the Baptist and his contemporaries from one side of the resurrection—the side that looked ahead to it. And we've seen how the actions and words of Jesus didn't seem to fit. Yet, they did, and it's the view from *after* the resurrection that shows us how. Wisdom

---

10 John 3:16, KJV
11 Mark 14:22, Luke 22:19, 1 Corinthians 11:23–24

is vindicated by her children, Jesus said. The results will verify the claims.

So what does the gospel look like, post-resurrection?

First, Jesus's resurrection means Yahweh actually did return to Israel. And as the New Testament tells the story, he didn't merely do so by speaking or working miracles through a human vessel like he did in Moses's time. Instead, he took on human flesh and came as a human being. When Isaiah said the Messianic king would be called "Mighty God, Everlasting Father"—well, it turned out to be a literal prophecy. When Isaiah said elsewhere that Yahweh would put on the garments of vengeance and do the work of deliverance and justice himself, without relying on human agents, that was literal too. What no one could have imagined happened. The Messiah wasn't just God's servant. He *was* God, intimately united with humanity forever. Jesus made the claim to be uniquely one with the Father in many subtle but ultimately undeniable ways.[12] *The resurrection means his claim was true.*

From the other side of the resurrection, the identity of Isaiah's Suffering Servant also became plain and clear, and it turned out that the Servant and the Messiah were one and the same after all. Jesus was despised and rejected, beaten and ultimately killed by men. He was, as Daniel and Isaiah both foresaw, "cut off." Yet his death was not the end. He was raised from the dead, and in so doing, he conquered not just human enemies but death itself.

---

12 Some of the more obvious are found in John 5:17–18, John 8:58, John 10:30–33, John 14:7–11, and Mark 14:61–62.

At the same time, as Isaiah foresaw, he somehow mysteriously bore the sins of the whole world in his body and destroyed them in the cross. With sins finally paid for and the debts of all humankind written off, Jesus rose from the dead to offer full and complete forgiveness on the basis of his own actions—and to offer life and a new covenant in his own body and blood. He became the long-awaited redeemer of Israel, offering freedom from the curse forever—but more than that. In the fulfillment of God's ancient promises to Abraham to bless all the nations through his seed, Jesus also effected forgiveness and redemption *for the entire world*. It wasn't only Israel, after all, that was suffering under the weight of sin and death. It was all of us.

So when we say there is forgiveness in Jesus, we aren't just saying we can have an inner feeling of peace and absolution. And we aren't just saying we can experience something good in the afterlife. We are saying that Jesus actually did something, in human history, that dealt with sin and made redemption freely available to us. Grace, which Paul identifies as the saving agent of the gospel, is God's leaning toward us, reaching for us—like a father bending down to take the hand of a small child and draw the child near. It's not just a nice thought or a metaphor. It's not just a reality in some subjective sense, some sense of inner peace or enlightenment attained through a philosophical approach. It's something Jesus *did*.

In his role as the Suffering Servant, Jesus also embodied and fulfilled the calling of Israel as a nation. This is a frequently missed point, but it's an important one.

We saw earlier that God, speaking to Isaiah, identified the Servant as Israel. Yet he also indicated that the Servant was not *all* of Israel but was a faithful person or remnant who would fully embody Israel's ancient calling and summon the whole nation back to God. This person would be an Israelite and would personify everything Israel had been called to be and to do. He would worship God faithfully, live a holy and devoted life, destroy the idols and evil powers of the world, and bring justice, mercy, and compassion to his fellow Israelites and to the whole world. He would love the law of God and carry it out authentically and fully. He would perfectly represent God as his "image" in creation and be a prophetic voice to the nations. All of these things, Jesus was and did. He was "the seed of Abraham,"[13] the Israel of God.

Jesus was also a king. We saw earlier that God entwined his own kingdom with David's when he made a covenant with David and promised to put one of his descendants on the throne of the kingdom of heaven.[14] Much like the wording of Isaiah 9, which gave the coming king names that sounded divine, this language seemed like a metaphor of some kind—just a promise to give David a long-lasting royal line and to bring justice through them. Of course, after David's family fell into apostasy they lost the throne, going into exile with the rest of the nation and never regaining their royal heritage. But Jesus, who was Yahweh enfleshed, was also fully human through his mother, Mary.

The early Christians formulated their belief in the

---
13 Galatians 3:16
14 1 Chronicles 17:14

nature of Jesus as fully man and fully God. One of the earliest confessions, which Paul preserved in his first letter to Timothy, reads:

> And without controversy great is the mystery of godliness: God was manifest in the flesh, justified in the Spirit, seen of angels, preached unto the Gentiles, believed on in the world, received up into glory.[15]

In the world's greatest sleight of hand, God kept his promise to David *and* placed himself directly on the throne. In Jesus, he eternally joined the kingdoms of humanity with the kingdom of God. This is a true fulfillment of the promises to David, but it is more than David himself likely ever imagined.

"Are you the One," John asked, "or do we look for another?" Jesus did not appear, to John's eyes, to be anointed to destroy the enemies of Israel and sit on Israel's throne, judging and ruling the nation and the world. But this is because John couldn't see the wider picture. In fact, John himself ceremonially purified Jesus by washing him in baptism, preparing him to begin his ministry.[16] As a Nazirite, John was unusually "clean"—unusually prepared for carrying out a ritual purification. And not long after John's death, Jesus was anointed with oil—anointed as the Messiah—not by a high priest or a powerful leader but by a disreputable woman overcome with emotion, who anointed his head and his feet with fragrant oil and then knelt down and wept on his

---

15 1 Timothy 3:16, KJV
16 David P. Seemuth, "Did You Realize You Are a Signpost?", posted at *N.T. Wright Online,* ntwrightonline.org/did-you-realize-you-are-a-signpost.

feet, kissing them and drying them with her hair.[17] People protested her action because it seemed so inappropriate, so scandalous. Then Jesus made the scandal even worse by connecting her act of worship with his coming death—and in a turn of phrase that must have seemed incredibly strange to everyone present, he connected his death with *gospel* or "good news":

> But Jesus, aware of this, said to them, "Why do you trouble the woman? For she has done a beautiful thing to me. For you always have the poor with you, but you will not always have me. In pouring this ointment on my body, she has done it to prepare me for burial. Truly, I say to you, wherever this gospel is proclaimed in the whole world, what she has done will also be told in memory of her."[18]

Jesus was the Messiah, foretold by the prophets and born to fulfill everything that was promised. Yet it was all so much more than anyone would have—*could have*—seen coming.

And it wasn't necessarily what many people wanted. They wanted their old expectation to come to pass, not this very different picture of fulfilment. If we are willing to get really, painfully honest with ourselves, we may have to admit this is the reason for some of our doubt too. We may not be willing to accept Jesus as he is, because who he is isn't who we want him to be. What he's

---

17 With slightly different details and emphases in each place, the story is told in Matthew 26, Mark 14, Luke 7, and John 12—one of very few stories to be repeated in all four gospels, a fact that underscores its importance.
18 Matthew 26:12–13, ESV

doing isn't what we want him to do. We can't control God or make him in our image, but we sure do have a long history of trying.

FROM THE THRONE OF HEAVEN TO THE HOLY SPIRIT

In the saga of Jesus's self-revelation as the Messiah, there are four distinct stages. Each one is needed to tell the story.

The first stage is the crucifixion. The second is the resurrection. In the third, ascension, Jesus revealed the mystery of the Davidic throne in the kingdom of God. Rather than taking the throne of earthly Israel, he ascended into heaven on the clouds, just as Daniel witnessed: as the Son of Man, Jesus "came with the clouds of heaven" and was seated at the right hand of God in the heavens.[19]

But no one saw that last part. The disciples saw Jesus go up in a cloud and were told by two angels that he would return in the same way,[20] but they did not see the heavenly coronation take place. They simply knew, from the prophecies of the Old Testament and from Jesus's parting words—"All authority has been given to me in heaven and on earth"[21]—that it was coming. So Mark's gospel ends with the words, "Then after speaking to them, the Lord Jesus was taken up into heaven and sat down at the right hand of God."[22]

---

19 Daniel 7:13-14. See also Matthew 26:64, Mark 14:62, Luke 22:69, Colossians 3:1, and Hebrews 8:1.
20 Acts 1:9-11
21 Matthew 28:18
22 Mark 16:19

But once again, God does not ask anyone to believe without reason. So this fourth, invisible stage of Jesus's Messianic ministry also had a particular earthly event associated with it. This event—the sign *on earth* that all these things had taken place *in heaven*—was the pouring out of the Holy Spirit on Jesus's disciples.

This fourth element in the story is important for two reasons. First, as I said above, it was the sign that Jesus had in fact been taken into heaven, given all authority, and seated at the right hand of the Father—events that no one on earth actually witnessed once Jesus had disappeared "in a cloud." When the Spirit was poured out on the early church in Acts 2, they understood it to be the sign that Jesus was Lord—that he had been enthroned in heaven. That's why Peter preached to his fellow residents of Jerusalem, who so recently had called for Jesus's crucifixion:

> God has resurrected this Jesus. We are all witnesses of this. Therefore, since He has been exalted to the right hand of God and has received from the Father the promised Holy Spirit, He has poured out what you both see and hear. For it was not David who ascended into the heavens, but he himself says:
>
> The Lord declared to my Lord,
> "Sit at My right hand
> until I make Your enemies Your footstool."
>
> Therefore let all the house of Israel know with certainty that God has made this Jesus, whom you crucified, both Lord and Messiah![23]

---

23 Acts 2:32–36, quoting Psalm 110:1.

But the Holy Spirit was not *only* a sign of Jesus's heavenly kingship. The Spirit's coming was also an important piece of the story in its own right—a pivotal piece of the mysterious plan God had set in motion when he first created the world. When the Holy Spirit came upon the Jerusalem believers, they went out in the street and preached the gospel in at least fifteen different languages, only one or two of which they knew. Other dramatic signs also accompanied the event. According to Acts 2:2–3, the sound of a violent wind filled the house where they were meeting, and visible tongues of fire appeared over each one of their heads. At least some of this must have been audible and visible to the people of Jerusalem as well, because it opened a door for Peter to explain it to them. Along with his claim that it was Jesus who had poured out the Spirit from heaven and that Jesus therefore must be seated in heaven, exercising authority over the earth, Peter also said the event was a fulfillment of ancient Jewish prophecy regarding God's dwelling with humanity:

> But Peter stood up with the Eleven, raised his voice, and proclaimed to them: "Men of Judah and all you residents of Jerusalem, let me explain this to you and pay attention to my words. For these people are not drunk, as you suppose, since it's only nine in the morning. On the contrary, this is what was spoken through the prophet Joel:
> And it will be in the last days, says God,
> that I will pour out My Spirit on all humanity;
> then your sons and your daughters will prophesy,
> your young men will see visions,
> and your old men will dream dreams.

> I will even pour out My Spirit
> on My male and female slaves in those days,
> and they will prophesy.[24]

Rather than a random event or simply a sign of something else, the coming of the Holy Spirit was the final piece of the puzzle. If you recall, God had promised to make a new covenant with his people in which he would dwell in them and with them.[25] He had promised to fill his future temple with glory.[26] But where in the past, the glory of God had accompanied God's entry into the buildings or tents constructed for him—often manifested as fire or cloud—*now fire and wind came and rested on human beings*. Where in the past the Holy Spirit had filled the temple in Jerusalem, now the Holy Spirit filled individuals. Where in the past God had confused the languages of humanity in order to divide them,[27] now he miraculously provided understanding in order to unite them. The holy ones, Daniel said, would receive the kingdom.[28] In this moment, they did.

Choosing to Know and Choosing to Love

Biblical faith, I said earlier in this book, is not a feeling or force we arouse within ourselves. It is always a response to a word or an event that is external to us. As Christians, we are not being asked to feel a certain way about God or about ourselves. We are being asked to ac-

---

24 Acts 2:14–18
25 Ezekiel 37:14, 27; Jeremiah 31:31–34
26 Haggai 2:7–9
27 Genesis 11:7–9
28 Daniel 7:18

cept that God has acted in history, and that his actions mean what he says they mean.

Dallas Willard points out that when it comes to the content of our faith, there are a handful of knowable facts. Creation and the resurrection both fall into this category. Creation is the only truly rational way to explain what we are doing here.[29] The resurrection is one of the best attested events of the ancient world and one of the most impactful—in real, quantifiable terms, totally external to our subjective experience of faith. And it is creation and resurrection more than anything that give our faith legs to stand on.

We have now found a firm basis for *knowing* that there is a vast nonphysical being underlying—perhaps also interpenetrating—the reality of the physical universe. We have pointed out that, although this is a knowable fact, no one *has* to know it. There are many people who do not know it. Either through neglect or resolve, they can refuse to seek out or attend to the considerations that would naturally lead to their knowing that there is a reality other than the physical world, one of magnificent proportions and intriguing character. The fact that some or many people do not know this or even deny it has of itself no bearing whatsoever upon whether it is knowable or whether some or many others do in fact know it.[30]

---

[29] Again, by "creation" I mean the fact that something that is *not* this universe and yet is capable of giving rise to this universe must have kicked off this universe at some point in the past, since every test, observation, and piece of evidence concerning the nature of this universe tells us it cannot have started itself.

[30] Dallas Willard, *Knowing Christ Today: Why We Can Trust Spiritual Knowledge* (New York: HarperOne, 2009), 117.

But we *can* know it. And if we can accept creation as a given, then we can take another step toward Christian faith, realizing that it is not, in and of itself, unreasonable. On the other hand, we could never arrive at Christianity through reason alone. Aristotle, thinking through the nature of reality in Ancient Greece and positing the existence of a First Cause, certainly did not come up with Jesus Christ. This is because Christianity isn't based on a philosophical construct alone; it's not just a *thought*. If God is truly outside of the created universe, then we can only know him if he reveals himself. Christianity is based on something that happened in history, on something that occurred within our material world that revealed God by his own choice and action. That something was the resurrection. And again, this is also the basis for believing that Christianity is *the* path, the exclusive way to God, and not just one option among many. Jesus made exclusive claims: "I am the way, the truth, and the life. No one comes to the Father except through Me."[31] If the Creator God resurrected Jesus, he validated those exclusive claims. No other religion can make a similar claim.

Ultimately, once we have settled the basis for Christian belief in our hearts and minds, we have a choice to make. This is so because there *are* also things we *cannot* know in the sense that we can't measure them or prove them through logic or science or historical evidence—things we simply do have to "take on faith." And interestingly, these things are almost always relational. We can't measure love; we can't catch integrity in a test tube.

---

31 John 14:6, NKJV

I suppose we can measure the effects of these things, but even then we have to take underlying motives and heart postures and the other's desire for relationship *on faith*. We have to choose to believe and to trust what the other tells us—what they speak and demonstrate, through action, of their inner nature.

These faith-based, relational things, it turns out, are what matter most to us as human beings. And we are designed and able to believe, even to *know*, these things. Despite our lack of *complete* knowledge, despite the fact that we could be wrong, every day hundreds of thousands of people vow their lives to one another in marriage. Every day friends choose to trust one another and to let one another deeper into their hearts and lives. Every day parents do their best by their children, and every day children tell their parents "Mama, I love you." "I love you, Daddy." This is the world we live in. It's a world where plenty of things can be measured, proven, nailed down by reason and evidence; *and yet it's a world where everything that truly matters stands or falls by faith alone.*

"We are saved by grace through faith,"[32] Paul wrote many years ago. As Luther styled it, "Grace alone by faith alone." It's a powerful formula but a simple one. Grace = the self-extension of God toward us, like a father bending to hold out his hand to a child. And faith = the only way we are capable of reciprocally relating to anyone. This is all that Paul is telling us, really: that God is calling us into a relationship with himself, and that in this relationship is our salvation.

---

32 Ephesians 2:8, paraphrase

The choice we make when we put our faith in God-in-Christ, then, is not the choice to know everything with absolute certainty, nor is it a choice to know nothing at all except by "blind faith." It's a choice to enter into a relationship, just as fraught as any other relationship we enter, except with the assurance that the Other in this relationship claims to be absolutely loving, perfect, and good, and that he has given plenty of evidence to back that up—not in our paltry lifetimes merely, but for thousands of years to billions of people, among whom you and I happen to be just one.

Chapter 10:
The Apologetics of Experience

My paternal grandmother, Lois Thomson, was the kind of woman who won arguments. She had a quick wit and a sharp mind and a strong will to triumph. In college she famously took a class or two on logic, and she never let anyone forget it (least of all my grandfather). And she appreciated apologetics. Both my grandparents loved to learn, and they collected books and videos defending the Christian faith from many angles, which they enjoyed sharing with their fifty-some grandchildren. But for all that, Grandma used to say that the strongest apologetic was personal testimony. "People can argue with anything you tell them," she said. "But when you look them in the eye and say, 'This is what God did for me,' *they can't look you in the eye back and tell you he didn't*."

Within Christian circles, the word *testimony* is usually employed to mean someone's personal story of encountering God, whether it's something as simple as an answered prayer or as profound as a transformed life.

Testimonies are vital to Christian communal life. They connect Christians within a congregation or community to what God is purportedly doing in their midst; they awaken hope and thanksgiving; and they serve as a horizontal corroboration and strengthener of faith. But it's no accident that the word is also used in legal contexts: in a courtroom, a testimony is the sworn statement of a witness concerning something they have seen or claim to otherwise know. (The word *testimony* comes from a Latin root meaning "witness.") A testimony, in other words, *is evidence*—to use Merriam-Webster's second definition, it is "firsthand authentication of a fact."

There is a logical progression in the reasons for faith I've been discussing. If the universe was created by a God and if that God is personal, we would expect him to become involved at some point in history. If he did become involved, and if he did so in Jesus and especially in Jesus's resurrection, and if he poured out the Holy Spirit into the world so he could be present and dwell among people who trust in him, then we would expect believers in Jesus to encounter God. And if believers in Jesus have encountered God, then we would expect evidence, of the only kind witnesses are able to give—we would expect firsthand authentication, or personal testimony of the presence and work of Jesus in their lives.

And in fact, we have that—or at least, millions of people claim we do. In my opinion, this is the most overlooked evidence for the truth of Christianity and of God in Christ. And I understand why: personal testimony is subject to all the problems that plague human perception generally and may have even led you or me to the point of doubt or crisis with which we are now wrestling. Experience by nature is subjective, our understanding of it is fallible, and yes, people can be led by their presuppositions and biases to read all kinds of meaning onto all kinds of events, whether that meaning is warranted or not. I'm certainly not immune to that, and neither are you.

And yet, we aren't the only ones with a story. From the very start, Christianity has been marked by testimony of the most remarkable kind. It has been marked by changed lives—from Paul, the once murderous Pharisee, preaching the Jesus he formerly persecuted; all the way down to the former addicts and alcoholics I have grown up knowing, who live clean lives of hope and purpose today. Christian testimony comes from people who are rich and powerful, and it comes from people who are poor and simple. It comes from doctors, lawyers, and professors, and it comes from four-year-olds and people with Down syndrome. Christian testimony comes from every corner of the earth, from east and west, north and south, advanced civilizations and tribal societies. Some of the most brilliant people in history have been Christians—and not just cultural Christians, raised within a certain worldview and never quite able to step outside of it, but Christians with a deep and personal faith based on personal encounter with God. Christians are comfortable and wealthy; Christians are persecuted, tortured, and martyred for their faith. Christians hold to many variations and shades of belief, but all ultimately stand on one thing—belief in Jesus, the Galilean, the man from Nazarene whose cousin John the Baptist asked him, "Are you the One, or should we look for another?"

Ultimately, they all speak with one voice—*and there are millions of witnesses*, stretching back in a straight line two thousand years to the resurrection of Jesus Christ. It's not even possible to list "prominent Christians" and come anywhere near a comprehensive list. As of 2001, the *World Christian Encyclopedia* claimed that an approximate 2.7 million people convert to Christianity every year, ranking it first—by far—in "net gains through religious conversion."[1] Does that prove Christianity is true? Of course not. But any argument made in court that was backed by the sworn testimony of 2.7 million witnesses would have to be given serious consideration—and that is only the number of people who annually come into the faith from another religion. Of course, not every convert has a personal story of encountering Jesus, or of personal transformation or answered prayer or some other powerful religious experience—but vast numbers of them do. And in fact, I suspect that this is unique, and that other religions and belief systems do not have the same kind of experiential backing that Christianity does.

I am sometimes struck, while reading the writings of people who lived hundreds of years ago in different times and cultures, by how much the Jesus they describe sounds like the Jesus I know. They write about what he whispered in their ear, and their stories all sound alike, and they all sound like mine. The Apostle Paul and Amy Carmichael and Catherine of Siena and me—we all know the same unseen Man. That seems extraordinary.

---

[1] See David B. Barrett; George Thomas Kurian; Todd M. Johnson, eds. *World Christian Encyclopedia* (New York: Oxford University Press, 2001), 360.

So I submit to you the notion that Christian testimony, throughout history and stretching well into the present day, constitutes a massive body of evidence that deserves to be carefully considered. I think my grandmother was right when she said you can't argue with someone who tells you what God has done for them—and when millions upon millions of people for thousands of years tell essentially the same story, their collective voice should not be ignored. Of course, quantifying and qualifying all of this testimony would be a massive undertaking, and to my knowledge no one has ever done it. But in your personal search for truth, I challenge you not to neglect this: Go and learn the stories of people who say they have been changed by Jesus. Track them down, buy them coffee, and listen to them. Dig out their stories in books and read them. And if you can, once you've gathered a sense of the weight and the number of them, explain them all away. In a sense this is how Jesus answered John. *The blind see, the lame walk, and the poor have the gospel preached to them.*

To reiterate: Christianity is not based on theories or philosophies or even moral teachings. It is based on claims that real things have happened in the real world. A domino fell, and that was creation. Another domino fell, and that was resurrection. These two events explain everything else. But it's true that we are at an enormous distance in time from the events of the Old and New Testaments, and that distance can create doubt. We didn't see creation happen. We didn't see Jesus come out of the grave. We *can* still see dominos falling, but of course we can find another explanation for that if we try.

(There is always a choice, so there is always the possibility of an alternative explanation.) So even though we can hear testimony and even encounter God for ourselves within the framework provided by creation and resurrection, this whole thing will always come down to making a choice. We like to demand absolute proof, but that isn't how this works; and at the risk of sounding like a broken record, that isn't how this works because this isn't about science, it is about relationship.

Of course, the irony is that even when we are given proof, it's usually not enough. There were people in Jerusalem who knew Jesus had been raised from the dead but chose not to believe in him. There were many people who saw his miracles, but rather than put their trust in God they just kept pushing for more and more miracles until it was clear their demands had nothing to do with faith at all but rather were an expression of unbelief. Given "proof," those who want to reject Jesus can always find an alternate explanation. ("He casts out demons by Beelzebub, the prince of demons," the Pharisees declared.[2]) Within relationship, demands for proof are a vicious cycle that can only be broken by a demonstration or a word of love, followed by a choice to trust in the heart behind them. Ultimately we are always asked to choose love and to choose trust.

If I may be very real here, I have experienced miracles. I have seen people healed. I have been rescued from death. I have had dreams and visions, I have had supernatural encounters, I have heard God speak, and I have experienced instantaneous personal transformation.

---

2 Matthew 12:24

And yet I am still capable of doubt, and I *do* still doubt. Sometimes I think I'm just crazy, and all of this has been my imagination. That's an alternative truth and a plausible explanation. It's not a *good* explanation, but it's there. And while in times of doubt it comforts and helps me to revisit the issues of creation and resurrection and the experience of millions of people who aren't me, ultimately this whole thing does come down to making a choice to believe, in the same way we believe in human love. Love can never really be proven, even though there are many good reasons to accept it as true: we just can't know one another's hearts that deeply. Love comes from the spirit, from the invisible part of us. Yet we can know it, experience it, and even stake our lives on it. I can look at you and say, "I love you." And you can choose to believe that is true—and in making that choice, absent of absolute proof, you can be absolutely right.

The Value of Experience

As I said earlier, testimony is vital to growing and strengthening our faith. But it's not just others' testimonies that matter; it's ours too. It's common today to think of "faith," "spirituality" or even "truth" as detached from the physical, historical world; as though spiritual things are fundamentally separated from material reality as we know it. But the Bible insists that this is not so—and that in fact, to draw up a map of the Christian faith as something detached from the world we live in is to discredit it completely. For Paul (always a good mapmaker), this is because the foundation of Christianity is a historical event: the resurrection of Jesus Christ. If the resurrection did not happen, he insists, we should all pack it up and go home.

> But if there is no resurrection of the dead, then Christ has not been raised; and if Christ has not been raised, then our proclamation is without foundation, and so is your faith. In addition, we are found to be false witnesses about God, because we have testified about God that He raised up Christ—whom He did not raise up if in fact the dead are not raised.[3]

But the resurrection is not the end of the story. There is a road from the resurrection to our present day, a road along which every other aspect of "the faith," and of our personal experience of it, falls into place. Dallas Willard says that for those who are willing to honestly consider it, the possibility of resurrection means that

> A reasonable next step would be openness to God's intervention in other contexts and, especially, in the events of their own lives today. Thus they could come to know the reality of a "spiritual life" for ordinary human beings.[4]

In other words, the historical fact of the resurrection provides solid ground for our personal, subjective experiences in the faith. I think it's important for us to really grasp this and recognize it, for two reasons: first because it gives us something external to ourselves that

---

[3] 1 Corinthians 15:13–15
[4] Dallas Willard, *Knowing Christ Today: Why We Can Trust Spiritual Knowledge* (New York: HarperOne, 2009), 136.

we can anchor to, which will help us avoid disillusionment when we get a smaller piece wrong; but also because it gives us reasonable grounds on which to accept spiritual experience as real. All too often our experience of faith is *not* grounded in much that is external to us, and it becomes very easy (and even reasonable) to doubt what we are experiencing in a subjective and internal way. If we mistake our subjective and internal experiences for "the faith that was once for all delivered to the saints,"[5] we make ourselves unnecessarily vulnerable to doubt. But at the exact same time, it is the external facts of Christianity that give validity to our internal experiences. Christianity at its best has always had a spiritual or "mystical" dimension,[6] and it is the historical events of creation and resurrection that give that dimension its reasonable foundation.

This matters very much to the whole issue of doubt. Some of us are doubting because despite our experiences with God, things are going sideways and causing us to question it all, including our experiences. If we're self-aware, we know that we are prone to confirmation bias and misinterpretation and yes, good old-fashioned flakiness. But others of us doubt because we have never experienced God at all, at least not in any way that we are

---

[5] Jude 3, ESV

[6] The word "mysticism" simply means "direct experience of the supernatural." Mystics are those who have such experiences, and Christian mysticism is distinct from the experiences of other religious groups in multiple ways. Throughout Christian history certain people have stood out as being especially notable mystics, but there is no reason to believe that mystical experience is not available to every believer. What we currently call the "Charismatic movement" is, in many ways, a widespread and popular experience of Christian mysticism.

aware of. I have experienced God a lot, but before I ever did, there was a long period when I did not. Before God spoke directly to my heart, he didn't. Before I ever had an out-of-the-box experience, all of my experiences were inside the box. In other words, just because you don't feel that you've ever experienced God doesn't mean you never will; and when we understand this whole saga of creation, resurrection, ascension, enthronement, and the pouring out of the Holy Spirit as the real-world basis for inner spiritual encounter and experience with God, we can open ourselves up for that kind of experience without fearing that we're losing our minds, becoming flakes, or straying into "New Age" territory.[7] Because of Jesus, it's reasonable to expect things to really happen that we can't explain in purely this-world terms. It's reasonable to expect heaven to invade earth in our own experience, because after all, it has already done so in the wider world outside of us.

For John the Baptist to doubt Jesus's Messianic identity, he had to doubt a lot of things he had personally experienced. He had to doubt the vision of the dove descending, and the voice from heaven, and the inner voice of the Spirit that had previously explained to him what the sign of the dove would mean. He had to doubt

---

[7] I have known Christians who fear any kind of spiritual experience, tending to ascribe it all to New Age or other influences in the church, but this fear is not founded in biblical teaching. We should exercise discernment and allow the Scriptures to give us our context for spiritual experience, but we don't need to be afraid of spiritual experience per se. Paul and John gave their simple litmus test in two statements: anyone (or any spirit) speaking by the Spirit of God will proclaim both "Jesus is Lord" and "Jesus Christ has come in the flesh." See 1 Corinthians 12:3 and 1 John 4:1–3.

the prophecies about his own life and the identity and calling he believed himself to possess and into which he had poured his whole life to that point. He had to doubt the whole schematic of his life and mission. In John's case all of his experiences turned out to be valid; he was right about all of it. But if John could experience God so vitally *before* the resurrection and before Jesus was enthroned in heaven; if he could know God so personally *before* the Holy Spirit was poured out with the promise that he would indwell, empower, teach, and fellowship with us, then we certainly have good reasons to expect to experience God as well.

In Matthew 11, after Jesus had finished rebuking those who stubbornly clung to unbelief despite many reasons to believe, he spoke first to the Father and then to the crowd:

> I praise You, Father, Lord of heaven and earth, because You have hidden these things from the wise and learned and revealed them to infants. Yes, Father, because this was Your good pleasure. All things have been entrusted to Me by My Father. No one knows the Son except the Father, and no one knows the Father except the Son and anyone to whom the Son desires to reveal Him. Come to Me, all of you who are weary and burdened, and I will give you rest. All of you, take up My yoke and learn from Me, because I am gentle and humble in heart, and you will find rest for yourselves. For My yoke is easy and My burden is light.[8]

Jesus's purpose in coming to earth was to reveal the

---
8 Matthew 11:25–30

Father to anyone who would choose to come to him. If we come to Jesus, we should expect to encounter God in personal and transformative ways.

THE LIMITS OF EXPERIENCE

At the same time, it's good and healthy to recognize the limits of our experience, precisely because we *are* human and subject to confirmation bias, misinterpretation, peer pressure, and just sometimes getting things wrong. I believe the Holy Spirit does speak to individuals and intervene in their lives. I believe he heals, does miracles, gives prophecies, answers prayer, reveals visions and dreams, and all the rest of it. I have personally experienced many of these things. But I also know that my own experiences of these things come through my personal filters, and therefore they are subject to interpretation (and reinterpretation), and in particular they are open to doubt.

The good news is, these experiences with God are not the foundation of my faith, even though they may be my entry point to it and central to my living it out. In my case this is very true. Although I grew up in a solid and faithful Christian home with exemplary Bible teaching and a good sense of apologetics, I did not really own my faith until I had a direct encounter with the presence of God at age thirteen or fourteen that changed my life. I knew the Bible prior to that but did not really *believe* it until I had "tasted and seen" God for myself. Even so, my memory of that moment is over twenty years old as I write this, and while it still strengthens me, it's not a sufficient anchor for my life. The whole foundation of *the* faith, built mostly on the resurrection, is.

Because it happened in the real, historical world, and because it happened outside of my spirit, my mind, or my experience, the resurrection grounds my faith in a way that no subjective experience ever could. In very simple terms, if I believe I've heard God say "turn left," and months or years later I decide that wasn't God speaking at all, or that I was mistaken in the way I heard the instruction, that does not have to shake my faith as a whole. Because my faith is grounded in the historical event of the resurrection, which does not change, I have freedom to stumble occasionally along the road opened up by that event.

In a way, this may be why John felt the inner freedom to ask the question he did. Notice that he still expected the Scriptures to be fulfilled, even if he had been wrong about Jesus: "Are you the One who is to come, *or should we look for another?*" John knew the prophetic Scriptures and believed them to be true, and because he had that foundation, he was able to question his own interpretations and experiences without completely losing faith in God.

It's the End of the World Again

When I was sixteen, the world had somehow convinced itself that at midnight on December 31, 1999, every digital clock in every computer and computer-driven system in the world would fail to roll over to 2000, and catastrophe would ensue.

At the time I was closely connected to a small Christian community in the Mojave Desert of California. We had a mandate to "love our neighbor" through practical means—food, water, clothing, and yes, disaster relief. At the same time that the news was predicting a potential societal meltdown, much of the church world was going predictably apocalyptic with the whole thing. Our community never quite bought into the "Jesus is coming back at midnight on New Year's Eve" thing, but we did prepare for the possibility that our neighbors would need us in a bigger way come January. We stockpiled water and canned food, took some disaster relief training, and just ... waited.

On December 31 the whole community gathered for a time of worship and prayer, which was our typical way of ringing in the new year anyway. The mood was curious and expectant, maybe a little apprehensive, but mostly just interested to see what would happen. We'd all heard the buzz. Maybe this would be the night after all.

Midnight arrived, every clock and computer in the world rolled over just fine, and in our little gathering, we held our collective breath for an instant while the lights stayed on, the fans kept running, and the night remained still. Then my friend Janet, who I think was helping lead worship and so had a microphone, said "Well, that was the biggest thing that never happened."

For us, this was no big deal. But there *were* groups that had convinced themselves Jesus was coming back, and/or that a disaster so large it would kick off the end times was in fact upon us. They had preached on it, prayed about it, and raised it to the level of gospel. Back in the 1980s the same thing happened (Jesus was supposed to return in 1988, and then 1989), and the same thing in the 1970s before then, when Chuck Smith of the large and influential Calvary Chapel movement fervently taught and believed that Jesus would return by the end of 1981. He was so clear and so adamant that many of his congregation gathered in his church on New Year's Eve, 1981, waiting for the Rapture to take place.

They were disappointed. More than that, some of their members experienced this disappointment as cause for their entire faith being rocked. Some fell away from Christianity entirely. Why not? Their leaders had preached that the end was at hand. Pastor Chuck had written convincing books on it, clearly showing how current events were "predicted" by the Bible.[9] And critics may point to this type of thing as evidence that Christianity as a whole is a sham.

But the truth is, the failure of a pet theory like this doesn't dismantle Christianity any more than the lack of a Y2K disaster means computers don't exist. Christian-

---

[9] It's easy to say that if we would just "read our Bibles" we could avoid this kind of thing, but I'm afraid that's not the case. Many of the beliefs we Christians adopt that turn out to be faulty are "based on the Bible." (And Calvary Chapel "reads the Bible" more thoroughly or faithfully than any other group or denomination I know of. One of their distinctives as a group is that weekly sermons usually work their way through the Scripture from Genesis to Revelation, skipping nothing. When they reach the end they start over again.) Humility helps us out here, as does acknowledging what the Bible is actually like. There are many things in it, *especially* those things having to do with eschatology (or "the study of last things") that are mysterious, symbolic, obscure, and sometimes deliberately difficult to understand.

ity is not built on pet theories. It's built on the resurrection and on everything the resurrection makes plausible and likely, including the present-day activity of the Holy Spirit in your life, my life, and your neighbor's life. We can fully embrace that and hold to it with absolute confidence even while recognizing that we are given to misunderstanding and embracing things that are, in retrospect, wrong or silly.

Nevertheless it *is* difficult when we believe something, or when everyone around us believes something, that turns out to be false. Peer pressure is powerful, and our desire for acceptance may cause us to accept things even if we're a little uncomfortable with them. We should all be careful to share our own pet theories with humility, recognizing the difference between foundational, resurrection-based truth and our momentary understanding of a passage or doctrine, or of something we believe God has said to us personally.

My pastor, Marc Brûlé, teaches that when the Holy Spirit communicates directly with us, there are three parts to that communication. First there is the information we receive: the actual picture, words, or impression. Then there is our interpretation of that information: the words we use to describe it and anything we may extrapolate from it. And finally there is our application of it: the actions we choose to take based on what we have seen or heard and then interpreted. This holds true for any type of experience with God or even how we initially understand Scripture. While the first element may come directly from God, the latter two involve our own understanding and so are very open to misunderstanding.

These kinds of experiences with God may be very real. They may be transformative. They are very much an outworking of the resurrection: they happen because Jesus was raised from the dead, ascended into heaven, and poured out the Holy Spirit on humanity as he promised to do. But they are not, in and of themselves, the foundation of our faith. That foundation is the resurrection of Jesus Christ in real human history.

This holds just as true for prophetic words, interpretations, or experiences conveyed to us by others. We can take these things as testimony, as evidence from a witness stand, even while recognizing that no human interpretation of events is complete and infallible. Even in the courts, this is true. There is no such thing as an eyewitness testimony that is completely reliable; our memories and perceptions just aren't that good. But that doesn't mean we don't use eyewitness testimony. In fact, we rely heavily on it—but we recognize its limitations. We do our best to place the testimony of any witness within a larger context that includes the character of the witness, corroboration by others, and surrounding circumstances. And finally we work with what we consider an acceptable rate of error. Jesus himself encouraged us to do this: while he did not promote judgmentalism as a rule, he did urge us to judge prophets and teachers by their fruit.[10] And Paul, speaking of the exercise of spiritual gifts (like prophecy) in a public church setting, wrote:

> Don't stifle the Spirit.
> Don't despise prophecies,

---

10 Matthew 7:15–20

> but test all things.
> Hold on to what is good.
> Stay away from every kind of evil.[11]

I say all of this because I think it gives us an important intellectual permission, or if you like, an important freedom for our souls: we are free to embrace Christianity 100 percent, taking in the entire road from resurrection to the present and active involvement of Jesus in our lives today through his Holy Spirit. Yet at the same time we are completely free to retain a healthy skepticism regarding certain claims made by others or even certain understandings held by ourselves. We are allowed to do this. It does not make us unspiritual in the slightest, nor does it amount to questioning God or abandoning our faith. It just makes us more sensible and humble Christians.

The Lord has asked us to be open to him and his Spirit. He has not asked us to throw our discernment overboard.

In the same Christian community where I lived in California, our founder was a very elderly woman of powerful and effective faith who was absolutely convinced that Jesus would come back before she died, *because he had told her so*. She died in 2010, and Jesus has not yet returned.

Early on I struggled with this a little, because—to be honest—in our context her word was often treated as though it came straight from the mouth of God. But I realized along the way that the struggle wasn't really nec-

---
[11] 1 Thessalonians 5:19–22

essary. She could be wrong, and I could still honor her, and that didn't actually change a thing about what I believe, including my belief that she did in fact hear from God clearly and often. I've come to realize over the years that many great Christians in many ages have claimed the same thing—that they personally would not die until the Lord's return, a claim they believed because "God told them." My theory is that God did tell them something having to do with his faithfulness to them and the way they would experience death. They just didn't put it into human words in quite the right way.

But even in recognizing the fallibility of human interpretation and understanding, and acknowledging the rather elastic way we navigate our relationships (including relationship with God), we can heartily value and seek out the apologetics of testimony, the evidence of personal experience—multiplied not by a few solitary witnesses, but by millions of them. Ultimately, a walk of faith is both internal and external, evidence and trust. It's a tension, and it will remain so until Jesus returns.

Chapter 11:
Wisdom Is Vindicated by Her Children

So now, after journeying through the history of Israel and the prophetic Scriptures, getting to know John the Baptist as a man and a prophet, and examining the reasons to take faith seriously in our own day—we are back where we started. Standing on a dusty Judean hillside under a hot desert sun, asking with John—*Are you the One who is to come, or do we look for another?*

We are back at the beginning, with our doubts and our questions. I hope this book has given us all permission to be honest about those and to face up to them, authentically and without pretense. John doubted. So, sometimes, do we.

After Jesus gave an answer to John's disciples, he turned to the crowds and said:

But what did you go out to see? A prophet? Yes, I tell you, and far more than a prophet. This is the one it is written about:

Look, I am sending My messenger ahead of You;

> he will prepare Your way before You.
> I assure you: Among those born of women no one greater than John the Baptist has appeared, *but the least in the kingdom of heaven is greater than he.*[1]

If John was inferior to you and me (who are now in the kingdom of heaven if we are followers of Jesus), it's clearly not because of any personal strength on our part or any weakness on his. It's instead a matter of positioning in history—of spiritual topography. John stood in a valley and looked up at mountain peaks hidden in clouds. We stand instead on the peaks, looking back at the valley, able to see it all from a higher vantage point. We are *greater than John* only in the sense of how staggeringly great is our position in the kingdom, as heirs and joint-heirs of the Son of God himself.

And so we're able to take as "common knowledge" things John could never even have guessed at. That Jesus was the Messiah, the Son of David *and* Isaiah's Suffering Servant, and that he conquered through his death. That the Messiah would not simply be a sign of Yahweh's return to Israel but would actually *be* Yahweh-in-flesh, God incarnate come to his people. That the enemy and oppressor to be defeated was not (in the final reckoning) the Roman Empire after all, but Death and Oppression themselves, as Jesus took up arms "against the rulers, against the authorities, against the cosmic powers over this present darkness, against the spiritual forces of evil in the heavenly places."[2] That Israel's sins *would* be forgiven in the atoning death of Jesus, but so

---

1 Matthew 11:9–11
2 Romans 6:12, ESV

would the sins of the whole world—the individual sins of every person, every family, every generation that has kept people apart from God. That Yahweh would return to his new temple in Jerusalem, but that temple would not be made of marble and wood and gold but of living stones, individual human beings in whose spirit God would dwell, linked together in a vast "house" built on the foundation of apostles and prophets and including both Jews and Gentiles in the plan of God.[3] And that the promises of freedom, prosperity, and peace in the promised land would extend out as well, becoming a promise of complete renewal for the entirety of earth and heaven as Christ came to "fill all in all"[4] and the glory of God truly "filled the earth, as the waters cover the sea."[5] So Paul calls Abraham not the "heir of the promised land," but "the heir of the world."[6] The promise of victory, life, fruitfulness, and blessing would extend into a promise of everlasting life in a marriage covenant with God, the great Bridegroom.[7]

Jesus did subvert John's expectations, and in fact the expectations of all Israel. But this subversion didn't make him less than what John expected. It made him much, much *more*. John had always seen pieces of the gospel, but he had never seen the whole. And the whole would mean salvation for us all.

So what about us? Even standing on our mountain peak, with excellent guides like Paul, Luke, John, and

---

3 1 Peter 2:5, Ephesians 2:19–22
4 Ephesians 1:23, ESV
5 Habakkuk 2:14
6 Romans 4:13. The Greek for "world" is "cosmos."
7 See Revelation 21–22.

Matthew to help point out the features of the land, we are vulnerable to doubt. The whole story has not come together yet. It turns out there is more to the road ahead; we have not yet reached the end. And our faith must be refined—purified and strengthened—if we are going to walk it to the finish line. Paul, who spoke so much about the mystery that had been revealed, also spoke about a mystery that is still hidden—and according to him, *we* are a part of that mystery. "So if you have been raised with the Messiah," he tells us in Colossians 3:1-4, seek what is above, where the Messiah is, seated at the right hand of God. Set your minds on what is above, not on what is on the earth. For you have died, and your life is hidden with the Messiah in God. When the Messiah, who is your life, is revealed, then you also will be revealed with Him in glory.

John the Beloved also spoke of a day when what is hidden will be revealed—specifically, when *we* will be revealed as we truly are, even as we see Jesus as he truly is.

> Look at how great a love the Father has given us that we should be called God's children. And we are! The reason the world does not know us is that it didn't know Him. Dear friends, we are God's children now, and what we will be has not yet been revealed. We know that when He appears, we will be like Him because we will see Him as He is.[8]

The New Testament is clear: the Messiah has come, but he is still coming. We are children of God, but we are still hidden. We are heirs now, but we have not fully

---

8 1 John 3:1-2

inherited. The kingdom is present, is *now*—and yet it is not yet.

Whatever we are going through today, we are still in the middle of the story. We have not yet reached the point when we can see the whole thing clearly. And until the day of full appearing, when Jesus is fully revealed and we are revealed along with him, there will always be things that don't seem to make sense.

The question is always: Whom will we choose to trust?

It's good to remember all that has happened so far—the story that begins in Genesis and continues into Jesus's day, and then on into ours. It's good because our story might be much like John the Baptist's. What was true for him may be true for us. If we are offended or disappointed in our faith, our disappointment may point *not* to a God who is less than what we thought, *but to a God is far more*. We find ourselves called not to hide from our disappointment, but to own it—and then to choose, rather than drowning in it, to lift up our eyes and see something bigger happening all around us. We are called to look not to our own interests but to the greater story of the kingdom of God.

In the end, truth is not just something we know. Truth is something we live out. *Wisdom is vindicated by her children.* Despite his doubts, it was ultimately vindicated in John. His life of sacrifice was not a waste. His bold declaration that Jesus was "the Lamb of God who takes away the sins of the world," that he was God's "beloved Son," and that he would baptize his people with the Holy Spirit and fire were all utterly true—more than John knew, in fact. John's work and message were vindicated in Jesus, who died—and then rose again and ascended "on the clouds" to heaven, where he was seated at the right hand of God just as Daniel saw in his Son of Man vision. John's faith and life were and are vindicated in the "holy ones," God's saints on earth, who have received the kingdom and who do the work, day by day, of filling the earth with that kingdom through the power of God's Holy Spirit.

And John will be vindicated in you and in me, if we stay the course—if we do not fall away, and if we are willing to allow the refiner's fire to do its work. *After all, the only way forward is through.* When the refiner's fire comes, there are only two choices: fall away, or press on. Ultimately, the wisdom of our choice will be seen in its fruit. And in the meantime, the fire will do its work of burning away much that was never of God to begin with, even while it purifies and strengthens that which remains.

John was certainly not the only follower of Jesus to experience the refiner's fire, although he was the first. Shortly before he died, Jesus said to Simon Peter: "Simon, Simon, behold, Satan demanded to have you, that he might sift you like wheat, but I have prayed for you that your faith may not fail. And when you have turned again, strengthen your brothers."[9] Reading between the lines of Peter's story, it seems as though his sifting, like John's refining, came through the clash between his expectations and Jesus's actions in reality. Peter even

---
9 Luke 22:31–32

seemed to have made peace with the idea of things going south in their ministry; he declared that he was willing to die with Jesus. When the soldiers arrived to arrest Jesus in Gethsemane, Peter put his money where his mouth was—he picked up a sword and went in swinging, one man against several hundred Roman soldiers and temple guards. Apparently they were caught off guard by Peter's courage, because he got the first blow in: he cut off a man's ear. But then Jesus stopped him, stooped down and picked up the severed ear, and miraculously reattached it to the man's head. Then he allowed himself to be arrested and taken away. From that point on, Peter's courage and faith alike began to unravel, until only a few hours later, standing in the temple court, he denied even knowing Jesus.

It was truly a crisis moment for Peter. One that went all the way to the place most of us fear reaching—the place of being so shaken in our convictions and afraid of the consequences that we are willing to deny Jesus. But for Peter, the moment of refining—hot as it was—ultimately purified and did not destroy him. As Jesus said, he did "turn again." And he strengthened his brothers, even becoming a rock of strength for the church of all ages.

> "From the days of John the Baptist until now," Jesus told the crowds, "the kingdom of heaven has suffered violence, and the violent take it by force. For all the Prophets and the Law prophesied until John, and if you are willing to accept it, he is Elijah who is to come. He who has ears to hear, let him hear."[10]

---

10 Matthew 11:12–15, ESV

The same charge goes out to us. If our faith is suffering violence, if circumstances are taking our convictions by force, Jesus's question is here to meet us at the brink: are we willing to accept that the story may be different than what we initially believed? Do we have ears to hear what God may be saying—can we cling to Jesus in personal trust without absolute certainty about every part of the story that surrounds us?

If we are doing battle with the spirit of the "Little Horn," whose words are arrogant and blasphemous and deceitful, let us take courage. The kingdom has been given to us—to you and to me, if we are in Jesus. And we will "possess it forever, yes, forever and ever."[11]

To Judgment and to Rest

Although it's not a popular subject in this day and age, judgment is a theme that runs throughout Scripture. The gospel has an edge; the message God speaks is living and active, and sharper than any two-edged sword. Jesus has come to gather his people to God, but in the process he has come to divide sheep from goats, truth from falsehood, belief from unbelief, believer from unbeliever. So Matthew 11 includes four verses we haven't discussed in detail in this book—four verses where Jesus pronounces judgment on those cities and towns that saw his miracles, heard the message John preached, and were given every reason to believe Jesus was the one God had sent—and yet rejected him.

> Then He proceeded to denounce the towns where

---
11 Daniel 7:18b

most of His miracles were done, because they did not repent: "Woe to you, Chorazin! Woe to you, Bethsaida! For if the miracles that were done in you had been done in Tyre and Sidon, they would have repented in sackcloth and ashes long ago! But I tell you, it will be more tolerable for Tyre and Sidon on the day of judgment than for you. And you, Capernaum, will you be exalted to heaven? You will go down to Hades. For if the miracles that were done in you had been done in Sodom, it would have remained until today. But I tell you, it will be more tolerable for the land of Sodom on the day of judgment than for you."[12]

Some people in Jesus's day, given every reason to believe in him, would not. As Dallas Willard has pointed out, there are many things we can know about God and about the truth—but no one *has to* know them. In the end it always comes down to choice. We choose to seek until we find. We choose to learn what there is to be known. We choose to trust.

We choose love.

In the end, the answer to doubt is not certainty, it is love. The spiritual fabric of the universe is relationship, and in relationship we cannot prove anything. We can only demonstrate, and we can only trust. *Proof* will not keep us here. In fact, if we continually demand proof, we will never really enter into love. Imagine a bride who cannot rest in her husband's love unless he somehow proves it to her, anew, every day. Imagine the cracks in that relationship as he realizes she does not trust him

---

[12] Matthew 11:20–24

and never will, because his efforts will never be enough to satisfy her doubt.

It's true that truth is not always easy to find. God has, in fact, hidden it—it is his good pleasure to reveal it to the seeking and to draw us into relationship with himself by the summoning power of that which is secret. We are invited to know and to understand. But ultimately, we will only reach knowledge and understanding by traveling through the questions, the doubts, the fears, and the challenges. We will gain it through experience, not merely through intellectual exercise. And we will not find assurance in nailing down every question but in encountering something of God, and from that place, learning to trust like children. We will choose to lay our doubts down, not because they have been satisfactorily answered (they can't be), but because we choose to love.

In that place, too, we will find relief and refreshing. We may even find healing—the kind of healing that enables us to trust more deeply. Few things are more intense than the refiner's fire, but even it is not the end of the story. On the other side is "turning again," repentance, strengthening, and *rest*.

> At that time Jesus said, "I praise You, Father, Lord of heaven and earth, because You have hidden these things from the wise and learned and revealed them to infants. Yes, Father, because this was Your good pleasure. All things have been entrusted to Me by My Father. No one knows the Son except the Father, and no one knows the Father except the Son and anyone to whom the Son desires to reveal Him. *Come to Me, all of you who are weary*

and burdened, and I will give you rest. All of you, take up My yoke and learn from Me, because I am gentle and humble in heart, and you will find rest for yourselves. For My yoke is easy and My burden is light."[13]

FINALLY: KEYS TO NAVIGATING OUR DOUBTS

When circumstances go sideways or long-submerged questions suddenly break the surface of our hearts, many of us will find ourselves facing the refiner's fire just as John did. I find comfort in knowing the fire is part of God's plan—that it has a purpose, not to destroy but to purify and to bring us into a place that is ultimately stronger, more secure, and more deeply bonded to our Lord. In the fire, the wrong beliefs and weak understandings we've held to burn away like chaff, and we ourselves are called into a deeper place of faith and trust.

But moments of crisis are never easy, nor does the word "moment" necessarily accurately reflect what you or I are going through. Although crisis itself is much like the relatively short period of transition during childbirth—excruciating to the point of nearly breaking us, but in itself designed to go fast and hard and then reach its goal and be over—doubts don't always manifest as crisis. Often they are gradual and compounding in nature. They can arise, build, and become a slow burn of torment for days or months, years or decades. To experience doubt does not make us lesser Christians. Jesus called John the Baptist "the greatest born among

---

13 Matthew 11:25–30, my emphasis.

women" at the exact moment of John's greatest doubt. He saw the faith and hope that ultimately underlay even John's questions. John wasn't doubting Jesus because he wanted the gospel to be false. He wanted Jesus to be the Messiah. He wanted it all to be true. But he needed to know that he hadn't built his faith on a false foundation. John cared enough about the truth to be willing to question it—to push it and make sure it really *was* true. We may need to do the same.

So the first step in navigating our doubts and surviving our periods of crisis is getting honest about our questions. Sometimes we avoid doing this because we think even *having* doubts is an affront to God; that it makes us like the Israelites in the wilderness who were so roundly rebuked for testing God. But there is an important heart-difference between doubting and testing God, and having questions and *seeking* him.

When you ask the questions because you care about the truth, when you knock on the door because you want it to be answered, when you seek God's face because you truly want to see him—then you don't need to be afraid of the fire that comes along the way. God—who became flesh in Jesus, suffered intensely, and cried out from the cross "My God, my God, why have you forsaken me?"—is not uncomfortable with raw pain or with unfiltered questions. He has felt them, and asked them, himself.

In the short term when we are dealing with doubt, then, we may need to remind ourselves of a few foundational truths. We may need to remember that we aren't crazy to believe what we do, even if the culture at large strongly hints that we are. There are reasons to believe. Creation, the resurrection, the testimony of millions of people throughout history who claim God is real, that he has spoken to them and interacted with them, and that they have been transformed as a result—these are good, solid grounds for belief. Not only that, but we have the testimony of Scripture and the innately compelling nature of the story it tells. And on top of that, we have our own experiences, our own testimony. But even then, let's remember the content of our faith that is external to us. We believe, not based on a single answered or unanswered prayer; not based on a powerful emotional moment during worship; not simply based on the powerful swell of belief from our immediate peers. Our faith, *this* faith—the Christian faith—is something much greater, older, and more established than that. It can be helpful, in times of doubt, just to remember that.

But ultimately, in the long term, let's surrender our need for control and for certainty and allow doubt to push us toward the truth we have not seen before. If we will press in to God, doubt gives us an unprecedented opportunity to ask bigger, better questions—to step back and see our lives, the gospel, and God himself from a bigger perspective. We may need to adopt new lenses, accept different time frames (usually longer ones), rethink the outcomes we are seeking, and even retool our identities. When the story we have told ourselves about God and our lives and our world is not working, we may need to ask—What if the storyline is different than I thought it was? What if there is *more*? What if rather than abandoning faith and abandoning God, we simply need to enlarge our understanding and trust to encompass something greater than we were able to see before?

As my friend Alan Gilman said, "It's time we learn to believe our beliefs and doubt our doubts." Sometimes that requires work, and asking more of our beliefs. Sometimes we need to dig deeper, work harder, learn more, and be willing to remodel our perceptions and our framework for the truth. In a treatise entitled *What's Wrong with the World,* the English writer G.K. Chesterton once wrote, "The Christian ideal has not been tried and found wanting. It has been found difficult; and left untried." When we are angry and hurt and frustrated by our perceptions of God, it may be worth asking if we are really being fair in our accusations or if we have left something untried, unasked, or unwelcomed. I've learned that if I read a story in the Bible (or more pertinently, in my own life) looking for a way to accuse God, I can probably find it. I can find a way to say God has failed in his promises, that he's abandoned me, that he's been unfaithful or unloving. But if I go in looking for a way to justify God and willing to call my own assumptions into question and compare them with the revealed truths of Scripture, I can usually find that too. Often the answer is simply, *Hold on. The story's not over yet.* In the garden of Gethsemane a moment after he'd tried to give his life to protect Jesus only to have Jesus rebuke him and go off willingly to be crucified, Peter felt like his world had collapsed. Three days later when he was greeted by the risen Christ, his world looked very different.

And in the meantime, while we are still struggling and wrestling in the darkness, the answers we seek are in the cross. God may not explain all our sufferings now, but he too has suffered. He has entered into our sufferings and borne them with us. He meets us in our weakness and brokenness, shares our pain, and promises to defeat the darkness through it. He fulfills and expands every promise of the Old Testament in the cross, and he does so subversively—defeating the enemy in his own death; paying for sins with his own blood; ruling the nations with kindness; bringing justice by bringing repentance, salvation, and regeneration. We may not understand everything, but the Jesus who suffered can be trusted. No, that can't be proven. But it certainly can be demonstrated, and it has been.

Ultimately we can't answer every question to our satisfaction on this side of eternity. Ultimately, when we've done the work, sought God, sought answers, and found what there is to find, we simply have to recognize that we are in a relationship and not in a math equation. We simply have to choose trust.

In the final reckoning, we will always have two choices. And once all the evidence has been considered, both choices will require faith. We can choose to reject God out of faith in some other story, or we can choose to trust him out of faith in the story told by the cross and the resurrection. In that story, it all comes down to love. God loves me, and I am asked to love him in return. He has proved nothing but demonstrated everything. I can know nothing with absolute certainty, but I can trust with my whole heart and life. In loving and being loved, the story will one day come clear.

In the final analysis, I don't believe because I can nail down the truth intellectually. That will always be impossible. In the final analysis, it is love that leads me to believe, and it is love that keeps me here.

I've made a point of stating, throughout this book, that we can't demand proof in a relational context. And it's true: we won't find peace or answers in some kind of formulaic, buttoned-up, here-it-all-is-on-paper absolute certainty. Yet there's another meaning to the word *prove*, one that is relational and experiential. It's the kind of proof that is only found after the decision to walk by faith. The old hymn exults:

> Jesus, Jesus, how I trust Him,
>
> How I've proved Him o'er and o'er,
>
> Jesus, Jesus, Precious Jesus!
>
> O for grace to trust Him more.[14]

I don't know where your journey will take you, any more than I know exactly where mine will end up. Maybe, when we have embraced questions and been willing to accept newer, bigger answers, we will lose everything.

Or maybe we will renew our faith and fall in love with Jesus, and the faith he gave us, all over again.

Personally, I think that is the more likely outcome.

---

[14] Louise M.R. Stead, "Tis So Sweet to Trust in Jesus." Written in 1882.

AT THAT TIME JESUS DECLARED,
"I thank you, Father, Lord of heaven and earth, that you have hidden these things from the wise and understanding and revealed them to little children; yes, Father, for such was your gracious will.

All things have been handed over to me by my Father, and no one knows the Son except the Father, and no one knows the Father except the Son and anyone to whom the Son chooses to reveal him.

Come to me, all who labor and are heavy laden, and I will give you rest. Take my yoke upon you, and learn from me, for I am gentle and lowly in heart, and you will find rest for your souls. For my yoke is easy, and my burden is light."

Matthew 11:25–30

Visit Rachel online:

Web: www.rachelstarrthomson.com
Facebook.com/RachelStarrThomsonWriter
Twitter: @writerstarr

Rachel Starr Thomson lives, writes, and drinks too much coffee in the Niagara Region of Ontario. She is an international speaker with 1:11 Ministries and the author of thirtysome works of fiction and nonfiction. Since 2015, she has blogged verse by verse through the gospel of Matthew at RachelStarrThomson.com.

THE SEVENTH WORLD TRILOGY

For five hundred years the Seventh World has been ruled by a tyrannical empire—and the mysterious Order of the Spider that hides in its shadow. History and truth are deliberately buried, the beauty and treachery of the past remembered only by wandering Gypsies, persecuted scholars, and a few unusual seekers. But the past matters, as Maggie Sheffield soon finds out. It matters because its forces will soon return and claim lordship over her world, for good or evil.

The Seventh World Trilogy is an epic fantasy, beautiful, terrifying, pointing to the realities just beyond the world we see.

"An excellent read, solidly recommended for fantasy readers."
– MIDWEST BOOK REVIEW

"A wonderfully realistic fantasy world. Recommended."
– JILL WILLIAMSON, CHRISTY-AWARD-WINNING AUTHOR
OF *BY DARKNESS HID*

"Epic, beautiful, well-written fantasy that sings of Christian truth."
– RAEL, READER

Available everywhere online or special order from your local bookstore.

THE ONENESS CYCLE

The supernatural entity called the Oneness holds the world together. *What happens if it falls apart?*

In a world where the Oneness exists, nothing looks the same. Dead men walk. Demons prowl the air. Old friends peel back their mundane masks and prove as supernatural as angels. But after centuries of battling demons and the corrupting powers of the world, the Oneness is under a new threat—its greatest threat. Because this time, the threat comes from within.

Fast-paced contemporary fantasy.

"Plot twists and lots of edge-of-your-seat action,
I had a hard time putting it down!"
—Alexis

"Finally! The kind of fiction I've been waiting for my whole life!"
—Mercy Hope, FaithTalks.com

"I sped through this short, fast-paced novel, pleased by the well-drawn characters and the surprising plot. Thomson has done a great job of portraying difficult emotional journeys . . . Read it!"
—Phyllis Wheeler, The Christian Fantasy Review

Available everywhere online or special order from your local bookstore.

FEARLESS

You can live free from fear.

Fear steals our lives from us. It steals our impact and cripples our joy.

In our modern world, there are a million reasons to be afraid.

But what if your default mode was courage and faith, not fear and timidity?

True freedom is possible—through the presence of Jesus and the practice of his Word.

In this book, we expose the insidious roots of fear and explore the answers found in the Bible. Learn how:

- THE FEAR OF THE LORD WILL BREAK THE POWER OF LESSER FEARS

- HOLINESS WILL CHANGE YOUR IDENTITY—AND GIVE YOU COURAGE TO STAND AGAINST THE TIDE

- THE PRESENCE OF GOD IS THE ANSWER TO THE WORLD'S TROUBLES

- YOU CAN PRACTICE THE GIFTS OF POWER, LOVE, AND A SOUND MIND

Available from Amazon and everywhere books are sold.

TIME TO ALIGN:
FREE EMAIL COURSE

Join Rachel Starr Thomson and the 1:11 team for a personal journey through 8 key areas of life in our free email-based course, "Time to Align."

This free, 11-week course is a spiritual recalibration: a chance to bring your heart, soul, mind, and strength into alignment with the nature and will of God.

To get your first lesson straight to your inbox, sign up here:

One11Ministries.com/Align

www.ingramcontent.com/pod-product-compliance
Lightning Source LLC
Chambersburg PA
CBHW030320100526
44592CB00010B/506